PRACTICAL *GARDEN* GUIDES

Conifers and Heathers

ALAN TOOGOOD

TIGER BOOKS INTERNATIONAL
LONDON

Editor: Pat Sinclair
Designer: John Fitzmaurice
Picture research:
    Moira McIlroy

This edition published
in 1989 by Tiger Books
International PLC, London

Reprinted 1990

Produced by
Marshall Cavendish Books Ltd
58 Old Compton Street
London W1V 5PA

ISBN 1 85501 004 6

Printed and bound in Portugal

CONTENTS

INTRODUCTION

Opposite A heather and conifer bed can look good all year round. This is an autumn scene, much enhanced by brilliant leaf colour from deciduous shrubs

Below Juniperus squamata 'Blue Star' is one of the bluest of the slow-growing, dwarf junipers and makes a superb specimen on a rock garden or in a gravel area

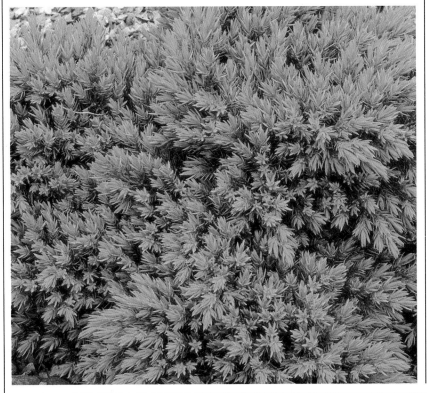

VISIT ANY GOOD garden centre and it is likely that a fair proportion of the area devoted to hardy plants will be taken up by conifers and heathers, such is the popularity of these two groups of plants.

What is a Conifer?

Generally conifers are cone-bearing trees, and shrubs, a good and well-known example being the pine. A cone is the seed 'container' and consists of woody, overlapping scales, protecting the seeds within. Some cones are highly ornamental, such as those of the cedars.

However, not all conifers bear cones: the seeds of yew, for instance, are partially enclosed in a berry-like 'container'.

The majority of conifers are evergreen, holding on to their leaves all the year round, but there are a few deciduous kinds, such as the European larch, which drop their leaves in the autumn.

The leaves of many conifers are needle-like, as they are in the pines and, indeed, they are correctly known as needles. Other conifers have scale-like leaves, often tightly overlapping, as in the Lawson cypress. Yet others — the junipers, for example — have short awl-shaped needles.

Most gardeners grow conifers not for their cones but for their attractive foliage and shapes.

What is a Heather?

Heathers are evergreen shrubs, generally low growing and mat forming, although some are tall, such as the so-called tree heaths (they do not actually grow into trees, but are simply tall shrubs). Some heathers have short needle-like leaves — the ericas — while others have tiny, closely set scale-like leaves — the callunas. The leaves of the daboecias are more like 'normal' leaves — elliptic in shape.

I have now mentioned the three genera that constitute the heathers: ericas, callunas and daboecias.

You will notice throughout the book that the term 'heath' is used as well as 'heather'. The two terms are used very loosely in gardening. Strictly speaking, the term heath should be applied only to ericas and daboecias, and the term heather to callunas.

4

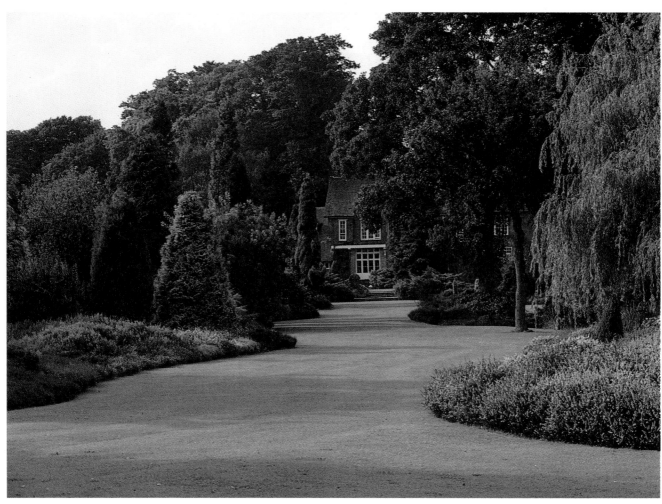

Above There are plenty of conifers available for grouping in large gardens, and large heather beds can reduce maintenance and provide all-year-round colour

Heaths and heathers are grown for their flowers, which in most are very freely produced and often last for many months. Some kinds, however, are grown primarily for their attractive foliage, which may be golden or shades of orange and red, often particularly striking in the winter. The dwarf or low-growing heaths and heathers make excellent ground cover.

Why Conifers and Heathers?

By now you may be wondering why I have combined conifers and heathers into one book. The answer is simple: they grow well and look superb together, a completely natural combination. As an example, in some parts of the country where there is natural heathland (maybe comprising calluna or ling) you may also find pines growing, generally the Scot's pine.

Both conifers and heathers like wide open spaces, such as moors and mountainsides — rugged countryside, in other words.

A mini-moor or environment which suggests mountain scenery can be created in the garden by planting a bed of heaths and heathers, interplanted with a range of attractive conifers, perhaps the dwarf kinds.

Are they good value?

I have already indicated that conifers and heathers are highly popular, so many gardeners must consider they are good value for money. Indeed they are, for conifers can live for a great many years. Heaths and heathers are also long-lived, but it should be said that after a time they are inclined to become straggly and to deteriorate in vigour. At that stage they are best replaced by young vigorous plants, but there is no need to buy in more plants: propagate your own from cuttings. They are easy enough to root.

Conifers and heathers are truly labour-saving plants for they need very little attention once planted. Of course, there is the inevitable weeding, and perhaps watering in dry spells, and most heathers benefit from a light trim over, but they do not demand much more attention than that.

Conifers look good all the year round, unlike many other shrubs, and you cannot really ask for more. Many heaths and heathers also have year-round interest, especially those with coloured foliage. A collection of different varieties of heathers will provide flowers all the year round, too, even in the depths of winter: indeed, the flowers are often found poking through a blanket of snow.

Are they suitable for your garden?

Whether you have acid (lime- or chalk-free) or alkaline (limy or chalky) soil, there are conifers and heathers to suit both. The winter-flowering heathers, for instance, grow well in chalky soils. If you have that type of soil and want to grow some plants that need acid conditions, you could, perhaps, consider growing them in ornamental containers of suitable compost.

Conifers and heathers like open conditions, not shaded and closed in with trees or buildings. They like the sun. That being said, there are a few exceptions among the conifers: some will thrive in shade.

You do not have to worry about the size of your garden, either. Even the tiniest plot can accommodate heathers — at least the low-growing mat-forming kinds, if not the large tree heaths. It can also take conifers, the dwarf-growing kinds, of which there are hundreds, many of them listed in the plant chapters later in the book. There are even some conifers suited to sink gardens, and it is impossible to garden on a smaller scale than that.

Very large gardens and estates could be enhanced by some of the giant conifers such as cedars. I have included some of the big trees in my lists, for there are gardeners who are fortunate enough to have an acre or two.

Will conifers and heathers suit the style of your garden? They certainly look at home in modern gardens, as is borne out by the extensive plantings seen on today's housing estates. They are suited to formal styles of garden as well as informal. Country gardens could certainly be enhanced by a bed of heathers, if not by the more formal types of conifer. They could have a place for some of the very informal-looking conifers — the yews, perhaps, or pines.

Some conifers, and most of the heathers, do not look out of place in shrub borders, so do not think that you have to grow these plants on their own.

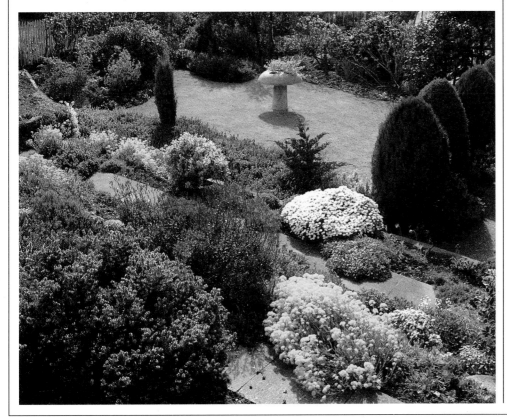

Left Heathers and dwarf conifers help to create extra colour and interest on rock gardens. There are varieties of both available for even the tiniest rock feature

CHAPTER ONE

MAKING A CHOICE

Opposite Chamaecyparis pisifera 'Filifera Aurea' is one of the favourite dwarf golden conifers for combining with heaths and heathers and also provides a marvellous texture

Below Juniperus sabina 'Tamariscifolia' is often used as ground cover and looks equally good when draped over a low wall

THERE ARE SO many varieties and species of conifers and heathers available, not only from garden centres but also from specialist nurseries, that many people will simply not know what to choose for their gardens. So let us take a closer look at what is available and consider the pros and cons.

Conifers

The dwarf conifers

I would suggest that people with small- to average-sized gardens opt for the dwarf conifers. Owners of large gardens could also grow them, but perhaps on a larger scale to create impact. It is difficult to give sizes, because they are so variable, but the dwarfs range from prostrate ground-cover plants, such as varieties of *Juniperus horizontalis* and *J. sabina*, to bushes in the region of 3m (10ft) in height, good examples being the popular *Thuja occidentalis* 'Rheingold' and *Chamaecyparis pisifera* 'Boulevard'. There are plenty of dwarf conifers in a range of heights between these examples, including *Juniperus communis* 'Compressa' whose ultimate height is about 1m (3ft). Many of the dwarf conifers are slow growing, in 10 years from planting gaining only about half of their ultimate height and spread.

A major attraction of dwarf conifers is their marvellous shapes, again extremely diverse. I have already mentioned that some are prostrate or mat forming, ideal for ground cover, whereas others are bun shaped: *Abies balsamea* 'Hudsonia' and *Picea abies* 'Gregoryana', for example. Others form neat cones or pyramids, such as the popular *Chamaecyparis lawsoniana* 'Gnom' and *Picea glauca* 'Albertiana Conica'. Yet others have a very narrow, columnar shape, and although eventually on the tall side, they take up very little lateral space and so are suitable for small gardens. A very well-known example is *Juniperus virginiana* 'Skyrocket'.

Another attraction of dwarf conifers is their foliage colours. They come literally in all shades of green, from pure greens (light, medium and deep), through grey- and blue-greens, to yellow, gold and bronze shades. Surprisingly, some of the dwarf conifers actually change colour in winter, many of the golden kinds becoming even more intense during the colder months. One of the 'bluest' dwarf conifers must surely be *Juniperus squamata* 'Blue Star', while one of the best golden

Above A group of dwarf conifers, contrasting well in colour, shape and texture, helps to 'soften' areas of paving and requires virtually no maintenance

gardens. There are many that are admirably suited to the rock garden, particularly some of the dwarf pines such as *Pinus mugo* 'Gnom' or 'Mops'. Do not think that dwarf conifers look out of place in the large garden: if you have space, plant each variety chosen in a bold group of several plants to give impact — say, three to five plants per group. There is scope, too, in a large garden for large drifts of ground-cover conifers, perhaps to cut down on the lawn area and thereby reduce mowing.

The larger conifers

The comments about shapes, foliage colours and textures apply equally to many of the larger-growing conifers. What is meant by larger conifers? There are no hard and fast definitions, but I would say that conifers that reach a height of over 3–4m (10–12ft) are in this category: *Chamaecyparis lawsoniana* 'Pembury Blue' and 'Winston Churchill' are very popular examples. Then there are the giant trees, such as *Araucaria araucana* (the monkey puzzle), *Cedrus atlantica* 'Glauca' (the blue Atlas cedar), *Larix decidua* (the European larch), *Metasequoia glyptostroboides* (the dawn redwood) and *Pinus nigra* (the Austrian pine).

Many of the larger conifers make superb specimen plants in a lawn, especially the cedars. Others can be planted in groups, for contrast in shapes, colours and texures.

Some of the larger conifers are used as windbreaks or tall screens, good examples being many of the tall varieties of *Chamaecyparis lawsoniana* (the Lawson cypress), x *Cupressocyparis leylandii* (the Leyland cypress), *Cupressus macrocarpa* (the Monterey cypress), *Larix decidua* (the European larch), *Picea abies* (the Norway spruce or Christmas tree), *Pinus nigra* (the Austrian pine) and *Thuja plicata* (the western red cedar).

Some are suitable, too, for creating formal hedges in gardens, both large and small. Popular for hedging are many of the varieties of *Chamaecyparis lawsoniana* (such as 'Green Hedger'), x *Cupressocyparis leylandii*, *Cupressus macrocarpa* and varieties, *Taxus baccata* (the common yew), *Thuja occidentalis* (the white cedar), *Thuja plicata* (especially variety 'Atrovirens') and *Tsuga heterophylla* (the western hemlock). Unlike such hedging subjects as

dwarfs is undoubtedly *Thuja occidentalis* 'Rheingold'.

Foliage texture is not, for some unknown reason, often considered by gardeners, yet many of the dwarf conifers are notable for their marvellous textures. Many have a soft feathery appearance: *Chamaecyparis lawsoniana* 'Ellwood's Gold' and *C. pisifera* 'Plumosa Aurea Nana', for example. Some have thin, thread-like foliage, as in *Chamaecyparis pisifera* 'Filifera Aurea'. The texture of many of the junipers is hard to define — often it is hard and prickly. A marvellous texture is created by many of the ground-cover junipers if they are mass planted: a far better choice than grass, in my opinion, for covering a bank. Grass, of course, is far more labour-intensive.

So, where are dwarf conifers to be used in the garden? Some ideas have already been given: they can be planted in a bed among heathers; they can be grown in groups on their own, for the sake of contrast in shapes, colours, sizes and textures; they can be grown with other shrubs in a border, and some of the smaller ones are ideally suited to tubs and other containers such as sink privet, conifers need very little clipping — generally once a year is sufficient.

Buying conifers

A reasonably wide range can be bought from garden centres in containers (such as pots or flexible polythene bags). Price depends generally on age — on how long it has taken the nurseryman to produce the plant. Very small plants of dwarf conifers, perhaps a couple of years old, will obviously be cheaper than larger plants about five years old. There is nothing wrong with small plants: you will simply have to be patient and wait longer for them to create an effective display. Certainly, though, the trend these days is for 'instant gardening', and there is a wide choice of larger, older conifers in the garden centres.

On the other hand, some conifers grow rapidly, so you can buy fairly large specimens for a modest price. This certainly applies to the conifers sold for hedging.

Conifers should be inspected closely before they are bought to make sure that they are of good quality and in a healthy condition. You should avoid plants with very dry compost, for drying out can eventually lead to leaf drop and the death of the plants.

Also to be avoided are conifers with brown scorch marks on the leaves. This could be due to wind damage, or, again, to drying out. After a hard winter some conifers in garden centres may look decidedly miserable, with browning foliage or leaves drying up. Brown, dead foliage at the base of plants could be an indication of disease, from which the plants may not recover. It should be borne in mind that once the foliage has died at the base of a conifer, it will not be replaced: the plant will have a permanently bare base.

The foliage, then, should look bright and healthy. If you are choosing conifers with coloured foliage, such as yellow or gold, make sure the colour is true: if the plants have been kept in shady conditions they may have lost much of their colour. Consider the shape, too. The cone, bun, globular and pyramid shaped kinds should be perfectly symmetrical, not with lop-sided growth (in other words, better-looking on one side than on the other). If plants have been packed closely together for some time they may lose their shape.

Conifers can also be bought, usually by mail order, from specialist growers, who generally supply a catalogue, perhaps with illustrations, certainly with descriptions. Specialists obviously supply a far wider range of varieties than garden centres, so if you want some of the more unusual or newer kinds, consider buying from a specialist.

Below Chamaecyparis lawsoniana 'Lanei' is one of the most popular of the larger golden conifers. It should be planted in a position which receives full sun

Heathers

Habits of growth

The habits of growth of heaths and heathers are not quite so diverse as those of conifers but, nevertheless, they do vary in size, shape, and in flower and foliage colour, so pleasing planting schemes can be created with these plants alone if you wish.

Heathers range from prostrate, ground-cover plants to large bushes. Among the most popular ground-cover types are undoubtedly the varieties of *Erica herbacea (E. carnea)*, one of the winter-flowering heathers. Many of the summer-flowering *Erica cinerea* (bell heather) varieties have a low, spreading habit of growth. Taller and bushier, but still low growers, are the varieties of *Calluna vulgaris* (ling), *Daboecia cantabrica* (St Dabeoc's heath), *Erica tetralix* (cross-leaved heath), *Erica vagans* (Cornish heath) and *Erica* x *darleyensis* (which flowers in the winter).

The taller kinds are popularly called

Below When planning a heather bed do not forget to include plenty of varieties with coloured foliage for all-year-round interest. Here a golden calluna provides colour

tree heaths and include *Erica arborea* (at least 3.6m or 12ft in height); *Erica australis* (about 1.8m or 6ft); *Erica erigena (E. mediterranea)* (about 1m or 3ft); *Erica lusitanica* (about 3m or 10ft); and *Erica* x *veitchii* 'Exeter' (about 2.4m or 8ft).

It cannot be said that there is a tremendous range of flower colours among the heaths and heathers. There are certainly many shades of pink, red and purple, as well as lavender, white and cream. A collection of heaths and heathers can, however, provide flowers for every month of the year. For spring there are most of the tree heaths, and some *Erica* x *darleyensis*, *Erica erigena (E. mediterranea)* and *E. herbacea (E. carnea)* varieties. Summer sees the flowering of varieties of *Calluna vulgaris*, *Daboecia cantabrica*, *Erica ciliaris*, *Erica cinerea*, *Erica tetralix* and *Erica vagans*. For autumn there are more varieties of *Calluna vulgaris*, and for winter further varieties of *Erica* x *dareleyensis* and *Erica herbacea (E. carnea)*.

The flowers of heaths and heathers do not vary a lot in shape: they are basically bell-shaped, and may be very tiny or, as in the daboecias, quite large. Some heathers carry their flowers in long or tall sprays, which are excellent for cutting to use in flower arrangements; good examples are the *Calluna vulgaris* varieties 'Alba Plena', 'Mair's Variety' and 'Serlei'.

Not only do heaths and heather provide masses of flowers, but many also have highly coloured foliage. These kinds provide colour all the year round, but it should be said that some do not flower too freely. Often the foliage changes colour with the seasons: in many the deepest or brightest colour appears during the winter. There are many *Calluna vulgaris* varieties, for instance, with colourful foliage, among the most popular being 'Beoley Gold', 'Blazeaway', 'Gold Haze', 'Golden Carpet', 'Joy Vanstone', 'Multicolor', 'Orange Queen', 'Robert Chapman', 'Sir John Charrington' and 'Sunset'.

Many heaths and heathers have attractive grey or silvery grey foliage, which contrasts especially well with the golden-leaved varieties. Among them are the *Calluna vulgaris* varieties 'Silver Knight', 'Silver Queen' and 'Sister Anne', and *Erica tetralix* varieties. Heathers with especially attractive foliage are indicated in the plant lists in Chapter Seven.

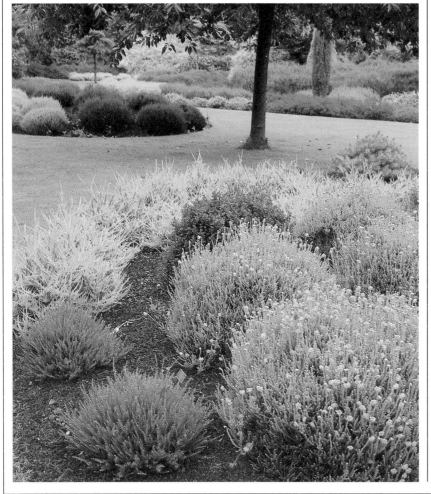

Even plain green foliage is attractive and there are many shades, from bright green, as in some of the tree heaths, to bronzy green, as in *Erica herbacea (E. carnea)* 'Vivellii'.

Uses in the garden

Generally heathers are mass planted in beds, several plants of each variety, to form bold groups. This provides a patch-work of colour all through the year. The low growers are used to form the patch-work and some of the taller kinds, the tree heaths, are planted to create height. Dwarf conifers are also used in a heather bed, again to create height, but also variation in shape, texture and colour. A heather and conifer garden is extremely labour-saving as the plants need the minimum of attention. Such a bed makes a particularly attractive feature in the modern open-plan front garden, but would be suitable for any other type of garden, too.

Heathers can also be grown with other plants, particularly shrubs. I like to see them used as ground cover around shrubs, one of my favourite schemes being winter-flowering heathers, plus some with coloured foliage, planted around shrubs noted for winter flowers and coloured bark. The winter-flowering kinds also look good around evergreen shrubs such as the laurustinus, *Viburnum tinus*.

Dwarf spring-flowering bulbs look good with heathers, too, particularly if they are planted so that they grow up through mats of winter-flowering heathers like *Erica herbacea (E. carnea)*.

Some plants, of course, do not look right with heathers. Included here are most of the herbaceous perennials, hardy and half-hardy annuals, and all the florists' flowers.

The rock garden can provide a home for some heathers. For instance, *Erica herbacea (E. carnea)* varieties do not look out of place with alpines.

There is no reason why some heathers should not be grown in ornamental containers such as tubs and window boxes, perhaps in combination with dwarf spring-flowering bulbs. Small, less vigorous heathers are recommended: *Calluna vulgaris* 'Golden Carpet', 'Kinlochruel', 'Multicolor' and 'Tib', and *Erica herbacea (E. carnea)* 'January Sun', 'Springwood Pink', 'Springwood White' and 'Vivellii'.

Buying heathers

As with conifers, many garden centres carry a reasonable selection of varieties of heaths and heathers. They are also sold in containers, such as pots or flexible polythene bags. Inspect plants closely before buying to make sure the compost is not dry and the foliage is not turning brown or drying up. You may prefer to buy heathers when they are in flower: being in containers, they can be planted when in full bloom.

You will find that sizes and prices vary. Heathers in small pots, available for very reasonable prices, are one-year-old plants. These are fine, and good value, although do not expect them to give an instant effect. Larger heathers are available: these are two-year-old plants and consequently more expensive. They will give a better effect immediately after planting, for they are of flowering size.

If you want a wider choice of varieties, and the opportunity to choose some of the newest on the market, then you will have to buy from a specialist heather nurseryman. There are several in the U.K. who operate a mail-order service. Some of our leading tree and shrub nurserymen also carry a wide range of varieties.

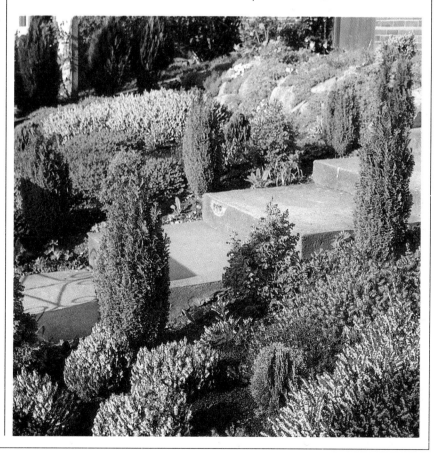

Below This front garden must certainly be labour-saving as it has been devoted largely to heathers and dwarf conifers. The season is spring, and the winter-flowering heathers are still in full flower

CHAPTER TWO

PLANTING AND CULTIVATION

Opposite Summer-flowering *Erica cinerea* 'E.G. Best', combined with the popular low-growing *Juniperus sabina* 'Tamariscifolia'

Below Groups of conifers should contrast in shape, colour and texture. There is literally no limit to possible combinations

A SUITABLE SITE is important. Heathers need an open, sunny aspect, free from shade and drips from trees, as they are plants of the wide open spaces. The majority of conifers need the same conditions. The golden conifers, especially, need maximum sun, otherwise their colour will not be so good. In shade, the golden conifers can lose all their colour and revert to green. The other conifers, such as those with green, grey or bluish foliage, will not mind some shade for part of the day. Some conifers, however, will grow in situations that receive little sun, examples being *Cephalotaxus harringtonia drupacea* (the plum yew), *Juniperus sabina* varieties, *Taxus baccata* (common yew), *Tsuga canadensis* 'Bennett' and *Tsuga heterophylla* (western hemlock). Details of suitable aspects will be found in Chapter Six.

You do not necessarily need a sheltered site for heathers and conifers, for most

are tough plants, often originating in open windswept areas. However, there are some that do not relish cold, drying winds and this is indicated where appropriate in the plant lists in Chapters Six and Seven. Some of the tree heaths, for instance, can be damaged by strong winds, as they have brittle stems. Very cold drying winds can damage young conifers but these can easily be protected, until established, as described later in this chapter.

Considering the Soil

Firstly, let us consider acid and alkaline soils. The former are free from lime or chalk and ideal for all heathers and conifers. If you have alkaline soil which contains lime or chalk, you can still grow heaths and heathers as there is a good range that will succeed in these conditions. You will be able to grow most conifers, too, although there are a few that will not tolerate chalk. Again, I refer you to Chapters Six and Seven.

How do you know whether your soil is acid or alkaline? Carry out a soil test with one of the inexpensive testing kits available from garden centres. You will find that full instructions are supplied.

Apart from acid and alkaline conditions, there are various soil types to consider. You may have a heavy clay type, for instance. This is suitable provided it is well drained, as the majority of conifers and heathers will not tolerate very wet or waterlogged soils. You may, therefore, need to carry out thorough cultivation if you have this type of soil.

The loamy soils are suitable, too, whether light, medium or heavy. The first two should be well drained, but heavy loam may need its drainage improved for heathers and conifers.

Sandy or gravelly soils are certainly well drained, so there is no problem here — indeed, many heathers and conifers are found growing naturally on these types of soil.

Finally, there are the peaty soils. These can be wet, but some heathers originate in these conditions and can therefore be grown. Choose those recommended for moist soils — see the plant lists in Chapter Seven. Conifers can be grown, too, provided drainage can be improved sufficiently.

Improving soils

If you have soil that is not too well drained, it pays to improve it as much as possible before planting, for most conifers and heathers need good drainage. The soil needs to be opened up and this can be achieved by digging in copious amounts of grit or coarse horticultural sand. Incorporate it into the trenches during digging (see below) and also mix it into the topsoil. Adding organic matter to the soil, as discussed below, will also help drainage.

Bulky organic matter benefits most soils, except naturally peaty types. Not only does it open up the soil and improve drainage, but it also acts like a sponge and conserves soil moisture during periods of drought. It is equally important that you do not let conifers and heathers suffer from lack of moisture. I therefore suggest that bulky organic matter is added to the trenches during digging and also mixed into the topsoil.

For heathers and conifers there is really nothing to beat peat — either sphagnum moss or sedge peat. Peat can be bought in bulk, which works out a lot cheaper than buying bales from a garden centre. Failing peat, use leafmould if available. Another good form of organic

Below Before planting heathers and conifers, you must find out whether your soil is acid (free from lime or chalk) or alkaline (chalky or limy). This is easily achieved by using one of the inexpensive soil-testing kits

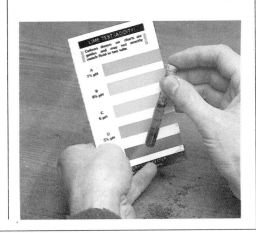

matter is pulverized or shredded bark, which lasts for a long time in the soil. Home-made garden compost can also be used, provided that it is really well rotted. This, of course, is the cheapest form of organic matter, for it costs virtually nothing.

Now to the hard work. Because conifers and heathers are long-term plants, it really pays to dig the soil thoroughly before planting, if only to incorporate organic matter and, if needed, grit or sand. You may get away with single digging (to the depth of a spade) if the ground is well drained, but if drainage is not so good, double digging is strongly recommended (this is breaking up the soil to two depths of the spade).

Before you begin digging it is advisable to kill off any perennial weeds, as it will be extremely difficult to control these once heathers and conifers have been planted: they are liable to grow up through the plants. Use a weedkiller containing glyphosate for perennial weed control, spraying it on to the growing weeds according to the maker's instructions. Once the weeds are dead, you can begin digging.

Single digging is simple enough. You start off at one end of the site by taking out a trench about (30cm) 12in wide and the depth of the spade, placing the soil near to where the last trench will fall. Then you add a layer of organic matter to the bottom of the trench. Take out the second trench immediately behind the first, throwing the soil forwards into the first trench. Again add organic matter. Proceed in this way until the plot has been dug.

Double digging involves taking out a trench 60cm (24 in) wide, and the depth of the spade, and once again depositing the soil near to where the last trench will fall. You then get into the trench and break up the soil to the depth of the spade (a fork may make the job easier). There is no need to turn over the soil — just loosen it thoroughly. Now add a layer of organic matter. Take out a second trench of the same dimensions immediately behind the first and throw the soil forward into the first one. Break up the soil in the bottom and add organic matter. Continue in this way until you reach the end of the plot and fill in the final trench with the soil taken from the first one.

If you are double digging a very large plot, you may find it easier to divide it into 1.2m (4-ft) wide strips, using garden lines, and to dig one strip at a time. You

Left Double digging is a good way of improving the soil. After breaking up the soil in the first trench, add organic material before topping up with the soil from the second trench

could work down the first strip, turn round and work back up the second, and so on.

The addition of organic matter and/or grit to the topsoil is most easily carried out after digging. Spread a layer over the surface and work it well in, using a fork, or perhaps a rotary cultivator for a large area. Ideally it should be worked into the top 30cm (12in) of soil.

After digging it pays to allow the ground to settle before planting. Soil which has been double dug will sink down quite a bit. Allow a couple of months, if possible, for settlement.

A few days before planting apply fertilizer to the surface of the soil at a rate of about 113g per m² (4oz per sq yd). I prefer to use an organic type of fertilizer for conifers and heathers, such as blood, fish and bone, or hoof and horn meal. The former does contain calcium or chalk, but only in minute amounts, so it will not harm those heathers and conifers that need acid conditions.

The fertilizer should be lightly pricked into the top 5–7.5cm (2–3in) of soil, using a fork. At the same time, break down the roughly dug soil until it is reasonably fine, and then firm it by treading systematically over the site with your heels. Carry out cultivation only when the soil is dry on the surface but moist underneath. Do not paddle around on wet soil or you will ruin the structure. Now all is ready for planting.

Planting

The optimum times of the year for planting conifers and heathers are April/May or September/October, as it is best to plant into warm soil. It will be warming up in the spring, and will still be warm in the early autumn. Warm conditions encourage new roots to spread through the soil quickly and so the plants establish rapidly. If you plant into cold soil — say, in the winter — new roots will not be produced, existing roots can die and rot off and the plants themselves may die. There is even more risk of this if the soil is wet as well as cold.

Planting can also take place from June to August, but bear in mind that during the summer the soil can dry out rapidly, so you must be prepared to water as often as necessary. If the soil is allowed to dry out, the young plants will suffer greatly and may die.

If you buy rootballed conifers (lifted from a nursery field) these should be planted only in April/May or September/October.

Before planting containerized or rootballed plants make sure the compost or soil is thoroughly moist. If necessary stand the plants in water almost to the rim of the pots or the top of the rootballs for an hour or so, remove and allow to drain, then plant immediately. The soil should ideally be dry on the surface but moist below when planting.

On no account disturb the rootballs when planting. To remove a plant from a pot, invert the pot, tap the rim on a solid object, such as the edge of a bench or top of a wall, and slide the pot off. If plants are in flexible polythene bags, carefully slit the bag down one side and underneath, using a knife, and peel it off. Rootballed plants have their roots wrapped in hessian or polythene. Simply untie and remove the material: ideally when the plant has been set in the planting hole.

Take out a planting hole with a spade or hand trowel, depending on the size of the plant, of sufficient depth that after planting the top of the rootball is only slightly below the surface of the soil.

If your soil is very poor you could use a proprietary planting mixture, consisting of peat enriched with fertilizers. Mix some into the bottom of the planting hole and into the soil which is to be returned around the plant. Work fine soil between the rootball and the sides of the hole, firming it with your hands (or heels for larger plants) as you go. When planting is completed lightly prick over the soil

Below Hedging conifers can be planted in a trench, fine soil being filled in around the roots and firmed really thoroughly by treading with the heels surface to remove footprints and relieve compaction.

As for plant spacing, you must allow sufficient space between plants for their ultimate spread, even though this may take many years to come about in the case of slow-growing conifers. In the intervening years the spaces between conifers can be filled with heathers or other low-growing plants, which can be gradually reduced in number as the conifers spread. In the plant lists I have given the spreads for conifers, so this will allow you to calculate spacings. The same applies to the large heaths and heathers. For the smaller heathers (the majority, in fact), I have suggested a suitable number of plants per m² (sq yd). Planted at these densities the plants will soon close up (within one or two years) and completely cover the ground.

Care after Planting

As with all plants, aim to get conifers and heathers established as quickly as possible, and try to avoid any possible setbacks or checks to growth.

It is important that you do not allow the soil to dry out after planting and this means keeping a close eye on the beds throughout the summer. As soon as the top 2.5cm (1in) or so of the soil has become dry, apply water. Watering should be gentle and thorough, so ideally use a garden sprinkler, of the oscillating or rotary type. You should apply enough water to penetrate to a depth of at least 15cm (6in). This means applying the equivalent of 2.5cm (1in) of rain, which works out at about 27 litres per m² (4¾ gallons per sq yd). This is easily measured by placing a few empty tins over the area being watered: when they have 2.5cm (1in) of water in the bottom you know you have applied enough. As a further check, about one hour after watering dig a hole about 15cm (6in) deep with a hand trowel: if the soil is still dry at the bottom, apply more water. Watering is best carried out in the cool of the evening when most of the water will go into the soil instead of evaporating.

Immediately after planting I like to cover the surface of the soil with a mulch of organic matter. A layer 2.5–5cm (1–2in) deep will be sufficient, but do not take it right up to the stems of the plants. A mulch should only be applied to moist soil. Its purpose is to prevent rapid drying out of the soil and suppress the growth of annual weeds.

One of the best mulching materials for conifers and heathers is peat, either sphagnum moss or sedge peat. Pulverized or shredded bark can also be recommended and I have found that it lasts much longer than peat as it decomposes less quickly. Both of these materials also create an attractive finish to a bed of conifers and heathers, and the plants show up well against them. Make sure the mulching materials are moist before spreading them over the soil.

Cold drying winds can be harmful to

evergreens immediately after planting. They cause the plants to lose moisture through their leaves quicker than they can take it up from the soil. Once they have put forth new roots, there is no longer a problem. Therefore, for the first six weeks or so after planting it is recommended that you spray the plants daily or twice daily with plain water, unless the weather is wet. The alternative is to spray the plants immediately after planting with a proprietary anti-transpirant spray, available form all good garden centres. Follow the manufacturer's instructions on use. Anti-transpirant sprays usually come in aerosol form, so they are easy to apply. They seal the foliage, which prevents rapid loss of moisture.

In the first winter after planting, conifers may need to be protected from cold winds, especially if your garden is exposed. Winds can 'burn' or 'scorch' the foliage of young conifers: it turns brown and dies off in patches. Once they are well established, however, you will not have this problem for the plants become tougher.

Conifers can be protected with temporary windbreaks. Set these up before the weather turns really bad — say, in mid-autumn — and remove them when conditions improve in the spring. Windbreaks should be erected on the windward side of the bed. Nothing elaborate is needed, just plastic windbreak netting, available from garden centres. This filters the wind and slows it down. The screen should be about 1–1.2m (3–4ft) high, the netting supported with stout bamboo canes inserted firmly in the ground 1–2m (3–6ft) apart.

Individual specimen conifers could be surrounded with a cylinder of windbreak netting, again supported with canes, and slightly taller than the plants.

I know that all this does not sound particularly attractive, but it is highly recommended, at least for the first winter, and particularly if your garden is in a cold, exposed area. It is far better to take these precautions than to lose expensive plants.

Regular Care

I have already said that conifers and heathers need the minimum of attention once they are established. If you mulch the beds, you will have few weed problems. If you do not mulch, you will have to hoe regularly between the plants to kill weed seedlings. Do not hoe deeply, as heathers are shallow rooting. On no account allow a dense growth of weeds, as this can retard the growth of the plants. If you first mulched the beds, top up the mulch in April each year if necessary, using the same type of material.

Conifers and heathers do not need heavy feeding, unlike some other garden plants, such as roses. I like to apply an organic fertilizer in April, such as blood, fish and bone, or hoof and horn. John Innes base fertilizer would also be suitable. A light application of 56–85g per m^2 (2–3oz per sq yd) is sufficient. Lightly hoe it into the surface of the soil or mulching material.

Watering should be carried out in dry weather as required, as conifers and heathers must not be allowed to dry out: this can cause loss of foliage and the plants may not recover. Heathers and some conifers are shallow rooting and therefore soon suffer in periods of dry weather if they are not watered, so do check the soil underneath the mulching material at regular intervals during dry weather.

Very little is needed in the way of pruning. Conifers do not need pruning, except for removal of any dead wood. If some of the taller conifers produce double leading shoots — in other words, if forking occurs at the top of the plant — one of these should be removed, as only a single leader is needed. This can be done in March or April.

Heaths and heathers need their dead flowers trimmed off each year. The dead flowers of callunas and summer-flowering ericas are often very attractive, turning to shades of brown and buff, and can therefore be left over the winter.

Right In the first winter after planting, conifers may need to be protected from cold winds. This is easily achieved by erecting a semi-permeable screen on the windward side

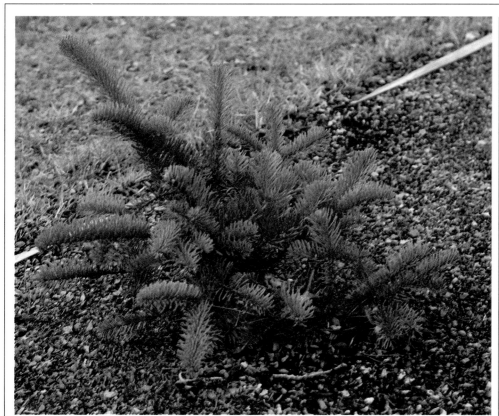

Trim them off, though, in spring, to just above the foliage. Never cut into the older wood of heaths and heathers. Use a pair of garden shears for trimming. The daboecias can also be lightly trimmed in spring. The winter- and spring-flowering heathers should be trimmed immediately after flowering, as described above.

Very few of the plants need staking after planting. However, one or two of the tall conifers might benefit from a stake until they are established and well rooted, particularly the cupressus. Staking, if required, is dealt with in the plant lists in Chapter Six. Tree heaths may need staking until established, particularly in windy areas. Nothing too elaborate is needed for heaths or conifers: a thick bamboo cane or perhaps a timber tree stake for larger conifers. Tie in with strong garden string or with proprietary buckle-type tree ties.

Fortunately, conifers and heathers are not troubled by pests but there are one or two diseases that might be troublesome. One disease that has reared its ugly head in recent years is known as phytoph-thora. It is a soil-borne disease and causes plants to die off from the base upwards. Often one side of a conifer will start to die — the foliage turns brown and dies. There is very little that can be done to control this disease: it is a case of digging up affected plants and burning them. The soil should be sterilized, and ideally, new plants should not be planted in the same piece of ground. There is no really effective soil sterilant available to the amateur; professional nurserymen use dazomet. However, you could try formaldehyde: it would certainly do no harm, provided that it does not come into contact with plants.

The other serious disease is honey fungus (*Armillaria mellea*). Again this is soil borne: it attacks the roots, runs up the stems and quickly kills the plants. If plants suddenly die for no apparent reason, suspect this disease. If honey-coloured toadstools appear around the base of plants in the autumn, the disease is confirmed. Bear in mind that honey fungus can kill large trees as well as young plants. Honey fungus is worse in some parts of the country than in others, especially in wooded areas. Dead and dying plants should be dug up and burnt and the soil sterilized with formaldehyde. There are one or two companies in the U.K. specializing in the control of honey fungus, so if this is a serious problem in your garden, it would be advisable to ask their advice. Sometimes, if the disease is treated in its early stages, plants can be saved. There are one or two products on the market specifically for the control of honey fungus: they are applied to the soil round ailing plants.

CHAPTER THREE

PROPAGATION

Opposite In autumn most of the summer-flowering heathers are over and the golden conifers are really coming into their own. Intensity of colour often increases as winter approaches

Right Conifers are propagated from semi-ripe cuttings which should be hard and woody at the base but still soft and green at the top

THE CHEAPEST WAY of obtaining new plants is to raise your own from cuttings taken from established plants. Cuttings of heathers, and of many of the conifers, root easily enough, in either a greenhouse or cold frame, and can be raised in a nursery bed.

Conifer Cuttings

The following conifers can be propagated from cuttings, but bear in mind that some varieties may not be easy to root. This especially applies to many of the golden conifers. My advice is to try. There is not a lot lost if some of your conifer cuttings do not root. Commercially the 'difficult' conifers are propagated by grafting, but this technique is not often used by the amateur gardener.
Cephalotaxus — September, greenhouse or cold frame.

Chamaecyparis — September/October, greenhouse or cold frame.
Cryptomeria — September/October, greenhouse or cold frame.
x *Cupressocyparis* — September/October, greenhouse or cold frame.
Cupressus — September/October, greenhouse or cold frame.
Juniperus — September to January, greenhouse or cold frame.
Metasequoia — hardwood cuttings, November/December, heated greenhouse.
Podocarpus — July/August, greenhouse or cold frame.
Taxodium — hardwood cuttings, November/December, heated greenhouse.
Taxus — August to October, greenhouse or cold frame.
Thuja — September/October, greenhouse or cold frame.
Tsuga — July to September, greenhouse or cold frame.

Conifers are propagated from semi-ripe cuttings (with the exception of metasequoia and taxodium which are increased from hardwood cuttings). The times of propagation are given above.

Semi-ripe cuttings are prepared from the current year's side shoots, which are soft or unripened at the top but ripe or woody at the base. The cuttings are prepared to a length of 10–15cm (4–6in) by making a cut immediately below a node or leaf joint, using a sharp knife. The leaves are stripped off the lower half, by either gently pulling them off or cutting them off with a knife. The base of each cutting must be well ripened and woody: it should have at least 12mm (½in) of brown wood. Dip the bases of cuttings in hormone rooting powder, as this will speed rooting and encourage a better root system. Only the lower 6mm (¼in) need be dipped in the powder. Tap off surplus powder as too much can damage the plant tissue.

Cuttings should be inserted in a cutting compost consisting of equal parts sphagnum peat and coarse horticultural sand — parts by volume. Use pots or deep seed trays, and insert the cuttings up to the lower leaves. Firm them in moderately with your fingers and water in with a rosed watering can.

As you will see from the above list, cuttings can be rooted either in a greenhouse or cold frame. Rooting will be quickest if you place the cuttings in a warm propagating case in a heated greenhouse. A mist propagator would also be suitable. Bottom heat will certainly speed up the rooting process.

You can also root conifer cuttings in an unheated greenhouse (or cold frame) but rooting will be very much slower: for instance, cuttings taken in late summer or autumn may not be well rooted until the following spring.

Cuttings should be shaded from strong sunshine and the compost must be kept steadily moist but not wet. Cuttings of some conifers may build up a large amount of callus or healing tissue at the base, which prevents rooting, so if you feel that some cuttings are not rooting, lift them and inspect for callus formation. If there is a large amount carefully trim it off with a sharp knife and reinsert the cuttings. x *Cupressocyparis* and *chamaecyparis* can develop a lot of callus.

When cuttings are well rooted they are lifted and potted off into 9cm (3½in) pots. Use a soil-based compost such as John Innes potting compost No. 1, or a peat-based type. Cuttings rooted in heat should be well hardened off in a cold frame before planting them out. Ideally, young conifers should be grown on for a few years in a nursery bed, so as soon as the pots are full of roots line out the plants in a spare piece of ground.

The best method of propagating metasequoia and taxodium is from hardwood cuttings in November or December, rooting them in a warm propagating case in a heated greenhouse. The current year's side shoots are used for cuttings, once they are completely hard and woody, which is after leaf-fall. Make the cuttings about 15–20cm (6–8in) in length, cutting above a bud at the top and immediately below a bud at the base, using sharp secateurs. Dip the bases in hormone rooting powder as for semi-ripe

Below left One should bear in mind that conifer cuttings can take many months to root. Rooting will be quicker if artificial heat can be provided, but slow in a cold frame

Below right Bases of cuttings should be dipped in hormone rooting powder before inserting them in a compost consisting of equal parts peat and coarse horticultural sand

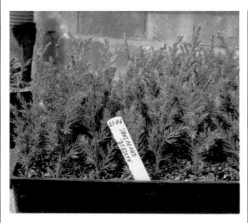

cuttings. Insert the cuttings to about half their length in pots of compost, water in and place in a heated propagating case. When well rooted treat like semi-ripe cuttings, by potting them individually into 9cm (3½in) pots.

Heather Cuttings

Heaths and heathers are also propagated from semi-ripe cuttings, during the summer, as soon as the side shoots are sufficiently developed. Actually, the propagation period can be spread over several months, so that you do not have to prepare all the cuttings in one go, and so that shoots can be gathered at the optimum stage of development.

Suggested times to propagate the major types of heathers are as follows:
Erica arborea, E. erigena (E. mediterranea), E. herbacea (E. carnea) and *E.* x *darleyensis* — May and June (take cuttings as early as possible).
Erica vagans — June (as soon as the stems are sufficiently long).
Erica ciliaris, E. cinerea, E. tetralix and summer hybrids — July and August (as soon as material is sufficiently long).
Calluna vulgaris and *Daboecia cantabrica* — August and September (take cuttings before growth hardens too much).

Side shoots are used for cuttings, pulled off with a heel of older wood. They should be between 3 and 5cm (1½ and 2in) in length. The leaves should be stripped off from the lower half of the cuttings, between finger and thumb. You should not attempt, however, to remove the leaves of callunas, for they are tiny scale-like leaves, and removing them would damage the cuttings.

I usually pinch out the tips of heath and heather cuttings, and it is certainly necessary to pinch out any flower buds that may be developing, as cuttings must not be allowed to flower: it sets them back and they take longer to develop into substantial plants.

Cuttings are dipped into hormone rooting powder as this speeds up rooting and ensures a strong root system. A suitable rooting medium consists of equal parts by volume of sphagnum peat and coarse horticultural sand. Heathers are best rooted in standard-sized seed trays. A comfortable number to insert per tray is a hundred. Make a hole for each cutting with a dibber and insert it up to the lower leaves. Firm in lightly with your fingers. When you have completed a tray, water in the cuttings, using a watering can fitted with a fine rose.

If you want quick rooting, place the cuttings in a greenhouse, in a heated propagating case, with a basal temperature of 21°C (70°F). A mist-propagation unit is excellent for heather cuttings, again provided it is equipped with bottom heat. Make sure the cuttings are shaded from strong sunshine or they may become scorched.

It is essential to keep the cuttings under mist or in the propagating case for only 14 days. If this period is exceeded, the cuttings will deteriorate and you may lose many of them. Rooting should be under way within this period. The trays of cuttings can then be stood on the greenhouse bench, and kept shaded.

Heather cuttings can also be rooted in a shaded cold frame, but they will take longer to root.

As cuttings become well rooted they should be potted off individually into 7.5cm (3-in) pots. Do not forget to use an acid or lime-free compost for those which need acid conditions, either loam-based

Left Cuttings of junipers can be taken in the period September to January, and may be rooted in a heated greenhouse or cold frame

Left Heathers are also propagated from semi-ripe cuttings, taken during the summer. They are inserted in a mixture of equal parts peat and coarse sand

Above A small amateur mist-propagation unit, ideal for rooting cuttings of conifers, heathers and many other plants

the autumn of the same year the rooted shoots can be lifted.

The parent plant must be completely lifted, with a spade or trowel, taking care to disturb the roots as little as possible. Try to lift with a good ball of soil round the roots. This is most easily achieved by cutting round the plant with a spade or hand trowel, some distance from the stems, and then cutting underneath the plant.

The plant should then be immediately replanted in a deeper hole, so that the lower third or half of the stems is buried. The stems should be well spread out while replanting, and fine soil worked between them. The soil should be firmed with your fingers as you proceed.

Little attention will be needed throughout the summer, apart from watering. It is essential to keep the soil steadily moist to encourage the stems to form roots.

In the autumn the plant is again lifted and all the rooted stems are cut off just below the roots. I prefer to pot off the rooted stems, rather than plant them direct in the open ground, as I feel they establish much better. They could be overwintered in a well-ventilated cold frame. I pot them off into 7.5cm (3-in) pots, using the compost recommended for heather cuttings.

Now you will have to make a decision about the parent plant: do you keep it or throw it away? All I would say is that it should survive and grow again if re-planted immediately. I generally cut back the remaining stems and as often as not new growth is produced in the spring. It is not a major catastrophy if the plant dies, however, for you will have lots of new young plants, which would set you back several pounds if you had to go out and buy them.

or peat-based. In fact, I prefer to pot all heathers into acid compost, even those that take alkaline conditions, as I feel that it gives them a better start in life; they seem to grow more vigorously. Pot the rooted cuttings only moderately firmly if using loam-based compost, and only very lightly if a peat-based compost is being used.

After potting, water in the plants thoroughly with a rosed watering can. Young heathers should spend their first winter either in a cold frame or in an unheated greenhouse, and kept well ventilated, except during very inclement weather.

They can be removed from the greenhouse or cold frame in April, as by then they do not need protection from the elements. I prefer to leave the plants growing in their pots until they are one year old, at which stage they can be planted out in their final positions. Do not forget to keep a close eye on water requirements while the plants are in pots, for these small containers can dry out very rapidly in warm weather. Ideally, they should be plunged to their rims in weathered ashes or sand to prevent rapid drying out.

Layering Heathers

Heaths and heathers can also be increased easily by a method of layering known as 'dropping'. It is a good way of obtaining a large quantity of new plants. Basically, it involves encouraging shoots to form roots while they are still attached to the parent plant.

Dropping is carried out in April and by

Summary

As I mentioned earlier in the book, although heaths and heathers are quite long-lived plants, they do start to deteriorate after some years, the length of time depending on variety. They start to look straggly and untidy and may not flower so freely, so it is worthwhile replacing older plants with young, vigorous specimens. As propagation is reasonably easy it is well worth raising your own replacement plants. If you propagate regularly each year you will have a constant supply of young plants. If you do not need them all, I am sure they would make welcome gifts for your gardening friends, or perhaps they could be exchanged for other kinds of plants.

Heathers from Seeds

Raising heathers from seeds is not often practised by amateur gardeners, but I feel that it is worth discussing, for there is increasing interest today in raising all kinds of plants from seeds, including wild plants.

Indeed, it is the wild species of heaths and heathers that are offered by some seedsmen, species such as *Calluna vulgaris, Erica arborea* and *Erica vagans.* Varieties (or, correctly, cultivars) are not raised from seeds, because they do not come true to type: they will not be identical to their parents in respect of flower colour and habit of growth. So, do not bother about collecting your own seed unless you have some of the true species.

If that is the case then it is best to collect your own, for heather seed has a short life, and it should be sown as soon as possible after collection. If you have to buy in seeds from a seedsman, sow them as soon as you get them, ideally in the summer or autumn.

Raising heaths and heathers from seeds is a slow process, cuttings or layering being far quicker, so you need patience.

Seeds are best sown in clay or plastic pans or half pots. Place a layer of drainage material in the bottom of these (such as crocks or broken clay flower pots), top with rough peat, then fill with peat-based potting compost. Sow the seeds very thinly. Do not cover them with compost as they are very tiny. Simply water them in with a watering can fitted with a fine rose.

The containers are placed out of doors in a cold spot, such as under a north-facing wall or fence, plunged to their rims in weathered ashes or sand to prevent the compost from drying out quickly. The compost must be kept moist at all times.

The seeds are over-wintered out of doors, and in the following spring they should ideally be transferred to a heated greenhouse, with a temperature of 7–10°C (45–50°F), in the hope of encouraging the seeds to germinate. Keep seedlings shaded from strong sunshine and make sure the compost does not dry out.

When you prick them out is up to you. Seedlings are very delicate and easily damaged, so you may prefer to wait until they are large enough to handle easily. I generally wait until they are about 5cm (2in) high. Even then, you have to be very careful not to damage the roots or stems, which are extremely thin.

Heather seedlings can be pricked out individually into 7.5cm (3-in) pots, using composts recommended for rooted cuttings. Water them in well after potting off and transfer to a well-ventilated cold frame. The young plants can be over-wintered in the frame and planted out when well established in their pots.

Below Young heathers can be planted in their final beds when they are one or two years old. Two-year-old plants give a quicker effect

CHAPTER FOUR

COLOUR THE YEAR ROUND

Opposite A heather and conifer scheme suitable for acid or lime-free soil, as it contains callunas (golden foliage) and summer-flowering ericas

Below One has to be very careful combining annuals with conifers and heathers, but this scheme, which includes bedding begonias and pink alyssum, works well enough

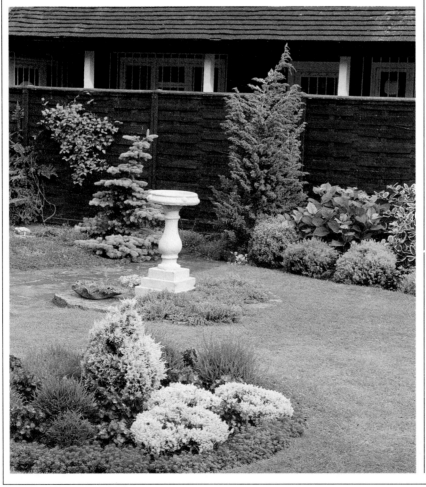

THE POSSIBILITIES FOR planting schemes featuring heathers and conifers are limited only by the imagination. It would be possible to draw up literally hundreds of planting plans for all-year-round features, all completely different. However, to get you started, I suggest a few fairly simple schemes here, suitable for small gardens. They feature some of the most popular heathers, conifers and other plants.

Heather and conifer island bed for acid or alkaline soils — Plan A

This scheme features the popular winter-flowering heathers, which will provide colour all winter and well into spring: the *Erica herbacea (E. carnea)* varieties 'Springwood Pink' (pink flowers), 'Springwood white' (white), and 'Myretoun Ruby' (ruby red). 'Foxhollow' (lavender), has bright gold foliage, providing interest all year round. Also for winter flowers are the *Erica* x *darleyensis* varieties 'Jack H. Brummage' (red-purple), 'Darley Dale' (pink), and 'Arthur Johnson' (rose-pink).

The dwarf conifers are attractive at any time of year. I have chosen the popular *Thuja occidentalis* 'Rheingold' (deep gold foliage), *Juniperus chinensis* 'Pyramidalis' (greyish or bluish green), *Chamaecyparis pisifera* 'Filifera Aurea' (bright yellow), and *Picea glauca* 'Albertiana Conica' (bright green).

This island bed, of informal shape, would look good in a lawn, or even in a paved or gravelled area. If you have the space you could have a group of, say, three island beds, with grass, paved or gravel paths between them.

Heather and conifer island bed — alternative for acid soils only

A similar island bed could also be created on lime-free soil only, by including a change of heathers. The heathers recommended below provide flowers mainly in summer and winter, although there could be some overlap into the other two seasons. There is plenty of foliage interest, too. The dwarf conifers, of

course, ensure colour all the year round.

There is quite a selection of heathers here: *Erica* x *darleyensis* '*Silberschmelze*' (white, November to April), *Calluna vulgaris* 'County Wicklow' (pink, August/ September), *Erica cinerea* 'Atrosanguinea Smith's Variety' (scarlet, June to September), *Erica herbacea (E. carnea)* 'Vivellii' (carmine, January to March), *Erica tetralix* 'Alba Mollis' (white, June to September, silver-grey foliage), *Daboecia cantabrica* 'Praegerae' (deep pink, June to October), *Calluna vulgaris* 'Robert Chapman' (purple, August and September, gold, bronze, red and yellow foliage for all-year-round colour), and *Erica vagans* 'Mrs D. F. Maxwell' (dark rose pink, August to October).

For extra height I would include *Erica erigena (E. mediterranea)* 'Brightness' with purplish red flowers from March to May. Dwarf conifers I recommend for this scheme are *Chamaecyparis pisifera* 'Boulevard' (silvery blue foliage), *Thuja*

occidentalis 'Rheingold' (deep gold), and *Picea glauca* 'Albertiana Conica' (bright green).

Dwarf conifer island bed for alkaline or acid soils — Plan B

Dwarf conifers on their own in an informal island bed create an attractive feature, again providing colour and interest all the year round. Once again, I would suggest creating the bed in a lawn or paved or gravel area and, if space permits, a group of three beds with paths between them. Each bed, of course, could be planned differently.

In this scheme I have aimed for contrast in foliage colour and texture, and in shapes of plants. The conifers come in a range of sizes, so this will not be a flat-looking scheme by any means.

All the dwarf conifers chosen for this scheme are popular and among the best

Below Plan A, heather and conifer island bed for acid or alkaline soils. Working in a clockwise direction, and starting at the '12 o'clock position', the plants are: *Erica* x *darleyensis* 'Jack H. Brummage', *Juniperus chinensis* 'Pyramidalis', *Erica herbacea* 'Springwood White', *Erica* x *darleyensis* 'Arthur Johnson', *Picea glauca* 'Albertiana Conica', *Erica herbacea* 'Myretoun Ruby', *Chamaecyparis pisifera* 'Filifera Aurea', *Erica* x *darleyensis* 'Darley Dale', *Thuja occidentalis* 'Rheingold', *Erica herbacea* 'Springwood Pink' and (centre) *Erica herbacea* 'Foxhollow'

available. *Juniperus horizontalis* 'Blue Chip' is prostrate in habit with brilliant silver-blue foliage, and contrasts beautifully with the deep gold cone of *Thuja occidentalis* 'Rheingold'. Next to this, and creating height, is the grey cone-shaped *Chamaecyparis lawsoniana* 'Ellwoodii'. The bright green cone of *Picea glauca* 'Albertiana Conica' contrasts well with the juniper 'Blue Chip' and with *Juniperus* x *media* 'Hetzii', which forms tiers or layers of almost horizontal branches, creating a flattish shape, with feathery grey-green foliage.

For height in the centre of the bed I have chosen *Juniperus virginiana* 'Skyrocket', a very narrow column clothed with bluish grey foliage. Although eventually quite tall, this juniper is still of a suitable size for a small garden as it does not spread. As a contrast in the centre of the bed is *Juniperus* x *media* 'Old Gold', which forms tiers or layers of horizontal branches, the overall shape being flattish, and bedecked in green-gold foliage. Around this juniper I have grouped *Juniperus conferta*, prostrate, forming dense mats of bright green foliage, *Thuja orientalis* 'Rosedalis', a pleasing dome shape, with very soft and feathery foliage, bright yellow in spring, light green in summer and purplish brown in winter, and the stunningly beautiful *Picea pungens* 'Globosa', bun or dome shaped, dense and bushy, with brilliant silver-blue foliage, at its best in spring and early summer.

Do make sure that this scheme is created in a sunny spot so that the golden conifers develop their optimum colour.

Below Plan B, dwarf conifer island bed for alkaline or acid soils. Working in a clockwise direction, and starting at the '12 o'clock position', the plants are: *Thuja occidentalis* 'Rheingold', *Chamaecyparis lawsoniana* 'Ellwoodii', *Picea pungens* 'Globosa', *Juniperus* x *media* 'Old Gold', *Thuja orientalis* 'Rosedalis', *Juniperus conferta*, *Juniperus virginiana* 'Skyrocket', *Juniperus* x *media* 'Hetzii', *Picea glauca* 'Albertiana Conica', and *Juniperus horizontalis* 'Blue Chip'

31

Schemes for conifers, heathers and other plants — Plans C and D

It cannot be said that heathers and conifers associate well with many other plants, but they can be used effectively with a wide range of ornamental shrubs and trees.

The planting plan (C) illustrated here is mainly for winter colour and interest and suitable for alkaline or acid soils. It could be part of a shrub border, or perhaps a special bed to create interest during the darker months.

The plan features a delightful ornamental small tree, *Prunus subhirtella* 'Autumnalis', the autumn cherry, with semi-double white flowers from November to March; the evergreen shrub *Viburnum tinus*, or laurustinus, with white flowers from late autumn to early spring; a witch hazel, *Hamamelis mollis* 'Pallida', with sulphur-yellow flowers in the period December to March; and a shrubby dogwood with bright crimson winter stems, *Cornus alba* 'Sibirica'. These shrubs form the background, and in front of them I have created a low planting, using *Cotoneaster salicifolius* 'Repens', an evergreen ground-cover shrub with small red berries in autumn, which contrasts superbly with the prostrate juniper, *Juniperus horizontalis* 'Bar Harbor', with greyish blue foliage, mauve-tinted in winter.

In contrast with this juniper, and with the evergreen foliage of the viburnum and the red stems of the dogwood, is the white-flowered *Erica herbacea (E. carnea)* 'Springwood White'. This is partnered with the rose-pink-flowered *Erica x darleyensis* 'Arthur Johnson'.

Planting plan (D) is mainly for spring and summer colour and interest, and for acid soil. It, too, could be part of a border. If you have a chalky soil you could still

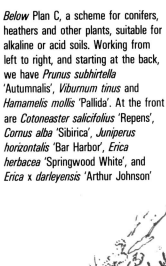

Below Plan C, a scheme for conifers, heathers and other plants, suitable for alkaline or acid soils. Working from left to right, and starting at the back, we have *Prunus subhirtella* 'Autumnalis', *Viburnum tinus* and *Hamamelis mollis* 'Pallida'. At the front are *Cotoneaster salicifolius* 'Repens', *Cornus alba* 'Sibirica', *Juniperus horizontalis* 'Bar Harbor', *Erica herbacea* 'Springwood White', and *Erica x darleyensis* 'Arthur Johnson'

use the birch, pine and genista, but you would need to choose lime-tolerant heathers (refer to the lists in Chapter Seven).

Birches look particularly good with heathers, so I have chosen the common silver birch, *Betula pendula*, with attractive white and black bark. Pines are also natural companions for heathers, such as *Pinus strobus* 'Nana' with silvery blue-green foliage. Gorse often grows with heathers and pines in the wild, so my choice here is *Ulex europaeus* 'Plenus', the double-flowered variety of the common gorse, with yellow blooms in April and May. I like to plant genistas with heathers, too, and have chosen *G. hispanica*, the Spanish gorse, with masses of yellow flowers in May and June. The heathers used here are *Calluna vulgaris* 'Elsie Purnell', rose-pink, August/September; *C. v.* 'Darkness', bright crimson, August/September; and *Erica cinerea* 'Golden Drop', with coppery gold foliage.

Specimen conifers as focal points

Conifers with particularly attractive shapes (and foliage colours) can be grown in isolation — say, in a lawn — perhaps to act as focal points in a garden (in other words, to lead the eye to various parts of the garden). When growing conifers in a lawn you should leave a circle of bare soil around them, and not allow the grass to grow right up to the stem, as this can retard growth, particularly in the early years of planting. Generally a circle about 1m (3ft) in diameter will leave sufficient space.

There are several dwarf (or at least narrow) conifers suitable for small gardens, including *Juniperus communis* 'Hibernica', *Juniperus virginiana* 'Skyrocket', and *Taxus baccata* 'Fastigiata Aurea'.

There are many tall or very large conifers that can be grown as single specimen plants in a lawn. Among those I particularly recommend are the abies, *Araucaria araucana*, cedars, *Chamaecyparis lawsoniana* varieties, *Chamaecyparis nootkatensis* 'Pendula', *Cryptomeria japonica* 'Elegans', *Cupressus macrocarpa* 'Goldcrest', *Ginkgo biloba*, *Metasequoia glyptostroboides*, *Picea brewerana*, *Picea omorika*, *Picea pungens* 'Koster', *Taxodium distichum*, and *Thuja plicata* 'Zebrina'.

Below Plan D, a scheme for conifers, heathers and other plants, suitable only for acid soils. Working from left to right, and starting at the back, we have *Betula pendula*, *Ulex europaeus* 'Plenus', and *Pinus strobus* 'Nana'. At the front are *Calluna vulgaris* 'Darkness', *Erica cinerea* 'Golden Drop', *Genista hispanica*, and *Calluna vulgaris* 'Elsie Purnell'

CHAPTER FIVE

MAKING THE BEST OF CONIFERS AND HEATHERS

Opposite Several conifers are suitable for planting and training as formal hedges. This neat hedge is formed of *Thuja plicata*

JUST AS HEATHERS and conifers are considered important as design features in many gardens, they are also highly valued for their use in meeting special needs. Conifers come into their own as screens, and wind-breaks, and, like heathers, make good ground covers. There is a wide range of plants to select from for containers, the greenhouse or the rock garden.

Conifer as Formal Hedges

A formal hedge is trained and clipped to a definite shape. It is neat, not too wide and therefore ideal for town or suburban gardens. Such a hedge can be grown to a height of 1.8–2.4m (6–8ft). There is no doubt that the best shape is a wedge, with the sides gradually tapering inwards to the top. Generally, the top is about half the width of the base, the latter being in the region of 1–1.2m (3–4ft). The reason for this shape is stability: the hedge will be very strong. Also, as the sides will receive maximum light, growth will be much better and thicker than would be the case with a straight-sided hedge. There is also less risk of snow lodging on top of the hedge. Bear in mind that a great weight of snow can split a hedge apart, so that it will never regain its original shape. Snow will be shed even more effectively if the top of the hedge is rounded rather than flat.

There is quite a wide range of conifers suited to training as formal hedges: *Chamaecyparis lawsoniana* and varieties such as 'Green Hedger', 'Fletcheri', 'Lanei' and 'Lutea'; x *Cupressocyparis leylandii* and its golden variety; *Cupressus macrocarpa* and its variety 'Goldcrest'; *Taxus baccata*; *Thuja occidentalis*, *Thuja plicata* and variety 'Atrovirens'; and *Tsuga heterophylla*. Descriptions of these will be found in Chapter Six.

With most of these conifers you can expect a growth rate of about 30cm (12in) per year, once the plants are well established, which may take a year or so. It will not take many years to achieve a 1.8–2.4m (6–8ft) high hedge. There is one conifer that grows even faster once established. This is x *Cupressocyparis leylandii*, which is capable of at least 60cm (24in) of growth per year. Some people consider this is too vigorous for a hedge, but I would not necessarily agree — I have a Leyland hedge and, like the others, it only needs cutting once a year, or at the most twice. I must admit, however, that I am on rather poor chalky soil and that may slow down its growth. At the other extreme, *Taxus baccata* is much slower, though when established it will grow about 15cm (6in) a year.

Below Yew, or *Taxus baccata*, has for hundreds of years been a popular hedging plant and it is not as slow growing as some people imagine

Growth rate does, of course, depend on soil conditions. If you have a very good, fertile soil, then growth will certainly be better than if your hedge is in poor soil.

Screens and Windbreaks

If you have a fairly large garden and want to hide an ugly view, or wish for complete privacy, then consider a tall screen of conifers. If you have a very exposed garden, you may well want a windbreak — again a tall conifer screen will serve the purpose.

A living windbreak is far better than a solid one, such as a high brick wall, for it filters the wind, thereby reducing its force. The wind rushes straight over the top of a solid windbreak and plunges down the other side, and such turbulence can cause a great deal of damage to plants.

A conifer windbreak will reduce the force of the wind for a distance of up to 20 times its height on the leeward side. Of course, there is one disadvantage in a tall screen or windbreak: it is not really suitable for small or average-sized gardens. You need the land to take it, for eventually it will be quite wide. It would look out of proportion in a smallish garden and could cast a great deal of shade. A tall screen will also take a considerable amount of moisture from the soil during the growing season and so the ground can become quite dry for several metres (yards) beyond it.

Conifers suitable for screens and windbreaks include *Chamaecyparis lawsoniana*, x *Cupressocyparis leylandii*, *Cupressus macrocarpa* and variety 'Goldcrest', *Larix decidua*, *Picea abies*, *Picea omorika*, *Pinus nigra* and *Thuja plicata*.

Preparation of Site

To prepare a planting site for hedges, dig a strip of ground 1.2m (4ft) wide, several months before planting, to allow for settlement. As a hedge is a long-term feature the soil should be double-dug as described on page 17. Before digging kill any perennial weeds with a weedkiller containing glyphosate, as they will be more difficult to control once the hedge has been planted.

The planting site for a tall screen or windbreak should be very much wider — double dig a strip 1.8–2.4m (6–8ft) wide.

Just prior to planting apply either a general-purpose fertilizer, balanced in nitrogen, phosphorus and potash, or a slow-release organic type, such as blood, fish and bone. About 113 grams per m^2 (4oz per sq yd) will be sufficient. Prick this into the soil surface, at the same time breaking down the roughly dug ground. Firm the site moderately well by treading systematically with your heels.

Planting

Planting times and methods have been given in Chapter Two, so there is no need to repeat them here. However, planting distances are very important in order to achieve a dense hedge or screen.

For formal hedges the following conifers are planted 45cm (18in) apart in a line: *Taxus baccata*, *Thuja occidentalis* and *Thuja plicata*. *Chamaecyparis lawsoniana* is planted 45–60cm (18–24in) apart, while x *Cupressocyparis leylandii*, *Cupressus macrocarpa* and *Tsuga heterophylla* are spaced 60cm (24in) apart.

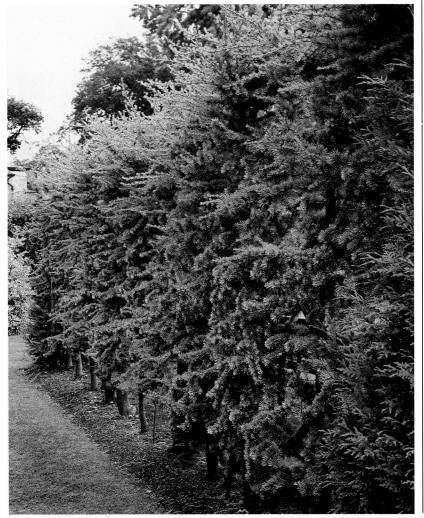

Below Not often thought of as being suitable for hedging, *Cedrus atlantica* 'Glauca' is nevertheless amenable to training and creates a most distinctive boundary

Generally, a single line of conifers is adequate for a formal hedge, but if you want a really thick hedge, plant a double staggered row of plants, spacing the rows 30–45cm (12–18in) apart.

Conifers for tall screens and windbreaks are spaced 1.8–2.4m (6–8ft) apart, in a single or double staggered row. Double rows should be spaced 1.8–2.4m apart.

Whether you are planting a formal hedge or a screen/windbreak, first put down a garden line to ensure a really straight row, and plant right up to this.

A word about sizes of conifers for hedges or screens. Do not be tempted to buy really tall plants for immediate effect, even though these may be offered by some garden centres and nurseries. They are slower to establish than smaller ones. I suggest that you choose plants 30–45cm (12–18in) high: not only will these establish much quicker, but they will also be a lot cheaper. You can, however, use either containerized or rootballed plants.

Aftercare

Some conifers used for hedging and screens/windbreaks may need to be supported after planting, until they are well rooted into the soil. This applies to those with shallow root systems, particularly x *Cupressocyparis leylandii* and *Cupressus macrocarpa*. *Chamaecyparis lawsoniana* may also possibly need supports to start with. Of course, this applies only to exposed or windy areas: if you have a very sheltered garden you may be able to get away without supports.

There are two ways of supporting the plants. Firstly, each can be provided with a stout bamboo cane, the height being about 1m (3ft) above soil level. The plants are tied into these with soft garden string as they grow. Alternatively, if you have many plants to support, you could rig up a horizontal wire, supported with posts, and tie each plant to this. Use strong plastic-coated wire or telephone wire, which can often be bought cheaply.

Supports should only be left in place until the plants are well rooted — in a year, or two years at the most. If you leave the supports in longer than this, the plants may come to rely on them and will not form strong root systems.

The initial training of a formal hedge is, of course, very important. Among gardeners there seems to be some dis-

agreement about whether or not to cut back the leading shoot of each plant after planting, to encourage really bushy side growth. However, I have never found this to be necessary with conifers, and so I leave the leaders until the hedge has reached the desired height. I recommend that the leaders are allowed to grow 15–30cm (6–12in) above the intended height of the hedge and are then pruned back to 15cm (6in) below this height. Pruning times are given later.

However, while the hedge is gaining height, the lateral or side shoots should be trimmed lightly each year (see trimming times below), as this encourages really dense growth. Remember to train the hedge to a wedge shape, as described earlier; trim the sides so that they gradually taper inwards from the base to the top. Generally, it is only necessary to lightly 'tip' the laterals while the hedge is gaining height. I must point out here that *Cupressus macrocarpa* and its varieties must never be trimmed hard at any time, for this can in fact kill the plants. So be prepared for a fairly wide hedge if you use this conifer.

Now let us consider the most suitable times of year for trimming conifer

Above A raised bed makes an ideal site for a collection of dwarf conifers and, of course, it would have the necessary free drainage

Below Formal hedges should be trained to a wedge shape and ideally have a rounded top. Such a hedge will be very strong, the sides will receive maximum light and the top will easily shed snow (which can split a hedge)

hedges, both for training and regular trimming:

Chamaecyparis lawsoniana and varieties — June and September.

x *Cupressocyparis leylandi* — May and June.

Cupressus macrocarpa — May and June.

Taxus baccata — June and July.

Thuja occidentalis — June and July.

Thuja plicata — June and July.

Tsuga heterophylla — June or August.

Remember that established conifer hedges generally need trimming only once a year, but if growth is rapid and you feel that a second trim is needed for the sake of a neat appearance, by all means carry it out, provided that it is within the times given above.

Tall screens and windbreaks do not need any form of training or subsequent pruning. However, if you spot any dead wood, this should be removed, the best time for doing this being April.

Formal conifer hedges can be trimmed either with garden shears or with an electric hedge trimmer. I must admit that shears make a better job of it. Electric hedge trimmers are inclined to cut partially through some of the shoots, leaving them hanging. Eventually they die and turn brown, which makes the hedge look rather unsightly. However, for really long hedges, automation is the sensible choice.

In order to achieve a really straight top to the hedge you should stretch a length of string along the top, at the height to which you want to trim; the string could be supported with some long poles or canes. When you are satisfied that the string line is really straight, start trimming to it. Nothing looks worse, in my opinion, than a formal hedge that varies in height along its length; it should be perfectly straight.

Many people ask whether conifer hedge trimmings can be composted. I always put mine on the compost heap, but do find that they take longer to rot down than some other softer materials.

I like to mulch a young hedge to help conserve soil moisture and to prevent weeds from growing. So, immediately after planting, I put down a 5–7.5cm (2–3in) layer of peat, leafmould, pulverized bark or very well-rotted garden compost and keep this topped up if necessary for several years until the young hedge is at the desired height. The same applies to tall screens and windbreaks. Remember that the soil must be weed-free before you put down a mulch and should be moist enough to sustain the plants.

It is absolutely essential to keep a newly planted hedge or screen well watered in dry weather. Again, I like to carry on watering until the hedge is fully developed. Once it has reached this stage it will, I find, survive dry periods. Use a sprinkler attached to a hosepipe to ensure that plenty of water is applied.

For the first six weeks after planting, I like to spray the plants with plain water daily to help them establish. Alternatively they can be sprayed with a proprietary anti-transpirant spray, which comes in aerosol form. Both these techniques prevent the plants from losing moisture rapidly through their leaves.

I like to give hedges and screens a supply of fertilizer in their first few years as I feel this ensures maximum growth. So, in the spring — say, in April — I apply an organic fertilizer, such as blood, fish and bone. This steadily releases plant foods over the growing season. The alternative is to use a balanced general-purpose flower-garden fertilizer. Apply at a rate of about 113g per m² (4oz per sq yd) along each side of the hedge or screen and lightly hoe it into the soil surface. If the soil is dry, it can be watered in as well.

It is also necessary to keep any young hedge or screen free from weeds. A dense carpet of weeds can seriously retard the growth of the plants. I have already mentioned that mulching is a great help here. Failing this, lightly hoe off weed seedlings, choosing a dry breezy day so that they quickly wilt and die; or use a chemical weedkiller such as paraquat or glyphosate, provided that you do not allow them to come into contact with the foliage of the conifers, for they will kill this as well.

An established hedge should be kept free from weeds too. It is a good idea to clear out hedge bottoms at least once a year. Ivy can be a problem in hedge bottoms and should be pulled out or it will grow up into the hedge. It may be better to pull out weeds that grow right in the middle of the hedge, rather than risk damage from weedkillers.

On no account allow tall plants to grow near a hedge, as they will reduce the amount of light that reaches it, and this results in weak, thin growth. Large shrubs, trees and so on should be positioned well away from hedges. You can grow dwarf plants fairly near to a hedge, but no closer than 60cm (24in).

Ornamental Containers

There is currently a great deal of interest in growing plants of all kinds in ornamental containers, such as tubs, large decorative pots, troughs, window boxes and sinks. It is an ideal way of growing plants in small gardens, as full use can be made of patios, terraces and other hard areas used for sitting or outdoor living.

Visit any large garden centre and you are sure to find a very wide range of containers in all shapes, sizes and materials. I suggest that you opt for deep containers for heathers and conifers, not the shallow bowl types which are inclined to dry out rapidly in warm weather. For instance, a good depth for tubs and ornamental pots is in the region of 45–60cm (18–24in).

Consider the materials carefully, too. Modern plastic containers do little, I feel, to enhance conifers and heathers, even though they are often used for the purpose. I much prefer containers in wood, terra-cotta clay, reconstituted stone, or even real stone if you can afford it. I suggest that you avoid glazed clay pots and tubs, for they are not porous and the compost in them could remain wet. I certainly use them, though, for other plants, such as summer bedding ones.

Growing alpines and other small plants, such as conifers, in sinks is very popular. Unfortunately, old stone sinks are extremely difficult to find and very expensive. The alternative is to use a glazed sink (which is deeper, and therefore better, in my opinion) and to cover it with hypertufa so that it looks

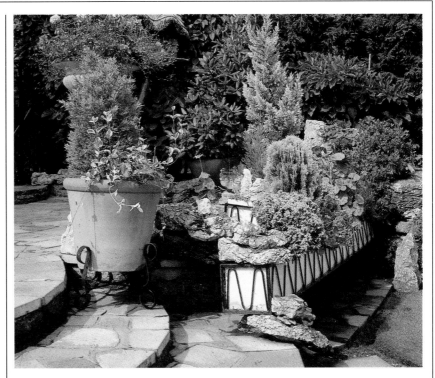

Above Many dwarf conifers are suitable for growing in containers on a patio, but of course you must keep a regular eye on watering

like natural stone. First the sink should be 'painted' with a proprietary bonding agent (as used in the building trade, and available from DIY shops). When this is tacky, a 12mm (½-in) layer of hypertufa mix is spread over it with the hands, leaving a fairly rough finish to resemble stone.

A hypertufa mix is made from two parts sphagnum peat, one part sand and one part cement — parts by volume. Add only sufficient water to create a stiff but pliable mix. If it is too 'runny' it will not adhere to the sink. When the hypertufa is dry and hard the sink can be prepared for planting.

Suitable plants

The following are some popular examples; further suggestions will be found in Chapters Six and Seven.

CONIFERS *Abies balsamea* 'Hudsonia'; *Chamaecyparis lawsoniana* varieties 'Ellwoodii', 'Ellwood's Pillar', 'Forsteckensis', 'Gnome', 'Pixie', 'Pygmy' (excellent for sinks); *Juniperus communis* 'Compressa' (superb for sinks); *Picea abies* 'Gregoryana' and 'Nidiformis'; *Picea glauca* 'Albertiana Conica'; *Picea mariana* 'Nana' (ideal for sinks); and *Taxus baccata* 'Fastigiata Aurea'.

HEATHERS *Calluna vulgaris* varieties 'Golden Carpet', 'Kinlochruel', 'Multicolor' and 'Tib'; *Erica herbacea* varieties 'January Sun', 'Springwood Pink' and

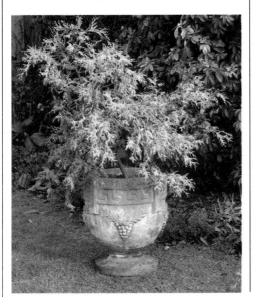

Left A pleasing choice of container for a golden thuja. One cannot go far wrong with classical designs in the garden

'Springwood White'. The heathers look particularly attractive in window boxes, perhaps with dwarf spring-flowering bulbs such as snowdrops, species crocuses, scillas and miniature irises.

Of the conifers I suggest one plant in a tub or pot (rather than a group), starting it off in a small pot and potting on as necessary as the plant grows. Specimens of the taller conifers in tubs, such as *Chamaecyparis lawsoniana* varieties 'Ellwoodii' and 'Ellwood's Pillar', and *Taxus baccata* 'Fastigiata Aurea', look attractive on either side of a front door, or they can be placed at the corners of a patio, for example.

Preparing and planting containers

It is essential that all containers have adequate drainage holes in the bottom, so do check before you add compost. Large containers are best set in position before you plant as they are, of course, heavy to move once they are filled with compost.

Sinks are generally raised 30–45cm (12–18in) above the ground, this being easily achieved with bricks.

A layer of drainage material must first be placed in the bottom of each container, about 2.5cm (1in) deep. Broken clay flower pots (crocks) make the best drainage material, but if this is not available use stones or shingle. Cover the drainage layer with a 2.5cm (1-in) layer of rough peat or leafmould to prevent the compost from washing down into the drainage and blocking it, preventing the escape of surplus water.

Several different kinds of potting compost can be used to fill containers. For conifers and plants in sink gardens (alpines/conifers), I prefer to use a loam-based compost, such as John Innes potting compost No. 2. Often the drain-age needs to be improved, however, especially for alpines, so I add about one-third extra of grit or coarse horticultural sand.

Heathers do well in peat-based or soilless potting composts, as they like peaty soils. They will grow well enough in John Innes No. 2. Do make sure that you use a lime-free compost for plants that must have acid conditions.

Several heathers can be planted in one large container, such as a tub or window box. I would recommend single specimens of conifers in each container, except in a sink garden, where you could have a group of, say, three plants. Start off conifers in pots and pot on until they are in larger containers. The plants do not like a large volume of compost round their roots: it can remain too wet and therefore roots may rot off.

Planting times have already been discussed in Chapter Two. The method of planting in pots and other containers is simple. With conifers, first place a layer of compost in the bottom and firm it moderately. It should be of a sufficient depth that, after planting, the top of the rootball is about 12mm (½in) below the level of the compost, and the compost surface is 12–25mm (½–1in) below the rim of the container, to allow room for watering. Set the conifer centrally in the container and trickle compost round it, firming as you go with your fingers. Water in well after planting.

Heathers come in small pots so they can be planted in the normal way after the container is filled with compost. Again, water them in thoroughly.

When planting a sink garden it is usual to fill it first with compost, leaving watering space. Generally, a conifer or group of conifers is planted in or near the centre, followed by alpines of various kinds, including trailing ones at the edge. A few small pieces of rock partially sunk in the compost complete the 'landscape'. The compost is then covered with a thin layer of stone chippings.

Aftercare

It goes almost without saying that a regular eye must be kept on water requirements, for containers can dry out rapidly in hot weather. You should not allow the compost to dry out but should apply water when the top 2.5cm (1in) or so of the surface has become dry. Watering should be thorough: apply enough so that it runs out of the bottom of the container; then you can be sure you have moistened the entire depth of compost. Lime-hating plants are best watered with rainwater if you have 'hard' or alkaline mains water.

Plants in containers will need more feeding than those in the open ground, for plant foods are leached out when watering. I like to give a topdressing of granular general-purpose fertilizer in the spring, lightly pricking it into the compost surface. During the summer I give an occasional liquid feed, using a balanced fertilizer, no more than about once a month for conifers and heathers. Feeding should cease in September.

It is unwise to allow the compost in containers to freeze solid during the winter, especially for prolonged periods, as this can result in the plants being unable to obtain sufficient moisture and, besides, the roots could be killed. It is a good idea, therefore, to insulate containers in the winter. This can be done by wrapping them with straw or bracken, held in place with wire netting.

Alternatively, it may be possible to move the containers into a frost-free (not warm) greenhouse during the hardest frosts.

If you start off conifers in small pots as suggested, you will need to pot them on regularly each year into the next size (or move them on two sizes) as they grow, to prevent them from becoming pot-bound (pots packed with roots), which stunts their growth. This can be carried out at the suggested planting times.

Conifers in final containers will need to have some of their compost replaced from time to time — say, about every two years, again at the suggested planting times. The plant should be removed from its container. This is most easily achieved with large plants if you can get someone to help you. Lay the container on its side: then, while you firmly tap the edges with a block of wood, the other person gently but firmly pulls the plant. The rootball should then slide out of the container.

As the container will be used again it should be washed out and allowed to dry. Some of the old compost should be teased away from the sides, bottom and top of the rootball — about 5cm (2in) if possible. Some of the roots can also be cut back. Then put the plant back in its container, filling in with fresh compost.

In the years between repotting or replacing compost, the plant can be topdressed with fresh compost in the spring. First scrape away about 2.5cm (1in) and then top up with fresh compost.

Heathers in containers, such as window boxes, I prefer to leave alone for several years until they start to look untidy and decline in vigour, when I replace them with young plants. All the old compost should be removed and discarded, re-filling with new compost.

In the Rock Garden

A rock garden should not be planted purely with alpines. A 'framework' of larger, woodier plants is needed, too. Many dwarf conifers are ideal for this purpose, planted singly or in groups of each variety, according to the size of rock garden.

If it is on a sloping site I prefer to plant low-growing conifers at the top and taller ones towards the bottom, as this creates a more natural effect: you do not see tall trees at the top of mountains, but rather lower down the slopes. On top are dwarf plants.

In the lists of conifers you will find a good range recommended for rock gardens. Among the best, in my opinion, are the following: *Abies balsamea* 'Hudsonia'; *Chamaecyparis lawsoniana* varieties 'Ellwoodii', 'Ellwood's Pillar', 'Forsteckensis', 'Gnome', 'Pixie' and 'Pygmy'; *Cryptomeria japonica* 'Vilmor-

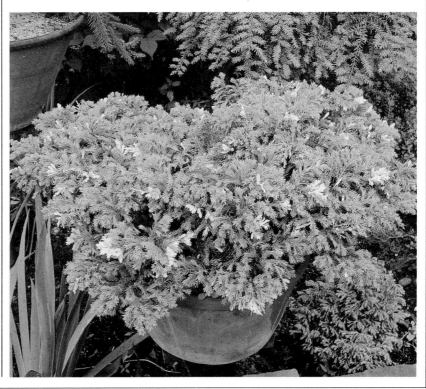

Below A pleasant contrast in colour — a terracotta pot containing the variegated *Juniperus* x *davurica* 'Expansa Variegata'

iniana'; *Juniperus chinensis* 'Japonica'; *Juniperus communis* 'Compressa'; *Picea abies* 'Gregoryana'; *Picea abies* 'Nidiformis'; *Picea glauca* 'Albertiana Conica'; *Pinus mugo* 'Gnom' and 'Mops'; and *Pinus sylvestris* 'Beauvronensis'.

Be selective as regards size — choose only the smallest for very small rock gardens and the larger ones where space permits, always bearing in mind the overall design of the site. Sizes will be found in the descriptive lists.

Some heathers can be grown on rock gardens and in my opinion those that seem most in keeping are the varieties of *Erica herbacea (E. carnea)*. The species itself is found on mountainsides in the wild, in pastures and on the edges of pine woods, and is, indeed, sometimes called the mountain heath, so it is an appropriate choice for rock gardens. It can be planted between rocks, for in the wild it is often found growing in cracks in the rockface.

As Ground Cover

One of the current trends in gardening is to plant areas of low-growing plants to completely cover the soil. This is known as ground cover. The purpose is not only to create an attractive area but to cut down on garden maintenance. Ground-cover plants generally need little in the way of attention and they suppress the growth of annual weeds, so you do not have to carry out soil cultivations.

It should be remembered, however, that before you plant ground-cover plants, all perennial weeds must be killed, with a weedkiller containing glyphosate, for the plants are not able to suppress these.

Prostrate or ground-hugging conifers are excellent ground-cover plants, for they have a dense habit of growth. They are also pleasing when mass planted, creating attractive textural effects.

Right An expanse of various ground-cover junipers, creates a superb textured effect, and cuts down on much labour

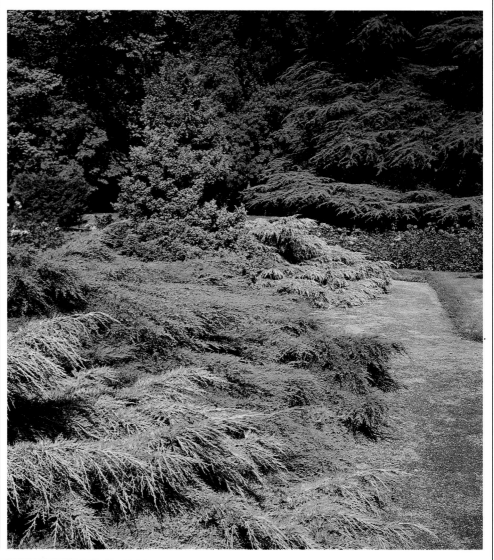

Many gardeners in the U.S.A. are particularly keen on ground cover and go in for it in a big way, often using conifers such as the prostrate junipers. They are planted by the acre, on motorway banks, in public gardens and parks, and round large public buildings, and what a marvellous effect they create — far more pleasing than acres of boring, closely mown grass.

I would also like to see far more use made of prostrate junipers in this country, not only in public places but in private gardens, even small ones, for it is possible to scale down the planting to suit any given area. Ground-cover junipers are particularly pleasing on a bank, for instance, where grass is all too often used, with possible difficulties when it comes to mowing.

Ground-cover conifers can also be used round larger shrubs in beds and borders: indeed, wherever you need to hide the soil and/or cut down on maintenance.

Some of the junipers in the descriptive lists in Chapter Six, are superb ground-cover plants. They include *J. communis* and varieties; *J. conferta* and varieties; *J. horizontalis* and varieties; *J.* x *media* and varieties; *J. procumbens* 'Nana'; *J. sabina* and varieties; *J. squamata* and varieties; and *J. virginiana* 'Grey Owl'. I also strongly recommend the golden prostrate yew, *Taxus baccata* 'Summergold'.

I have indicated the spreads of these conifers in the descriptive lists, so these will give you an idea of planting density. In practice I would plant a little closer than the ultimate spreads as this will give a quicker cover.

It may be advisable to prune some ground-cover junipers to ensure a really dense habit and to keep them shapely. For instance, any over-long shoots should be cut back, otherwise they will spoil the overall effect. Carry out any pruning needed with secateurs, in the spring or summer.

Ground-cover junipers do not have to be grown alone: you can grow other ground-cover plants with them to create a pleasing tapestry. In this instance I would suggest bold informal patches of each type of plant, in a random pattern.

I consider the most effective ground-cover plants to grow with junipers are the prostrate, evergreen cotoneasters. These produce masses of berries in the autumn, in various shades of red or orange, contrasting superbly with the foliage of the junipers.

There are many prostrate cotoneasters to choose from, but some of my favourites are 'Coral Beauty', orange-red berries, shiny leaves; *C. dammeri* with orange-red berries and long trailing stems; *C. dammeri radicans*, which is similar but with shorter leaves; *C. microphyllus*, tiny glossy leaves but large scarlet berries; *C. microphyllus cochleatus*, a slower grower, otherwise similar; *C. salicifolius* 'Gnome', with a mound-forming habit; *C. salicifolius* 'Parkteppich', masses of small red berries; *C. salicifolius* 'Repens', masses of small red berries, small narrow leaves; and 'Skogholm', large coral-red berries, tiny leaves and vigorous spreading habit.

Some of these you should be able to find in a good garden centre, otherwise it is a case of buying by mail order from a specialist shrub nurseryman, or even from a ground-cover specialist — there are now several in the U.K.

A fairly recent introduction is a prostrate firethorn or pyracantha, which I have found to be a good companion for junipers. Called *P.* 'Alexander Pendula', it is vigorous, completely prostrate and carries masses of orange berries in the autumn. I actually found some plants in one of our well-known garden centres, but you may have to hunt around for this variety.

Similar to a prostrate cotoneaster is *Stranvaesia davidiana undulata* 'Prostrata', with red berries in the autumn and wavy-edged evergreen leaves. Like the cotoneasters and pyracantha, this plant is very adaptable as regards soil and aspect. Happily, the birds leave the berries alone, which is not always the case with cotoneasters and pyracantha.

Above Abies procera 'Glauca Prostrata', a prostrate form of the noble fir. Very slow growing and ideal for a rock garden or mixed group of small conifers

In the Greenhouse

In these days of high fuel costs, more and more people are deciding not to heat their greenhouses over the winter. They either close them down and forget about them for six months of the year, or go in for plants that can be grown without heat during the winter. These are, of course, hardy plants, such as spring-flowering bulbs, coloured primroses, polyanthus, or vegetables such as winter lettuces.

Other gardeners go in for alpines, which flower in winter and spring. They need no heat and indeed demand plenty of ventilation while they are under glass. They are generally grown in pans and kept in cold frames for most of the year, plunged to their rims in ashes or sand to prevent rapid drying out. The frames are sited in a sunny part of the garden and the glass lights are only put on between October and April to keep off the winter rains. The plants are supplied with plenty of ventilation throughout the winter. The alpines are taken into the cold greenhouse as they are coming into flower and

returned to the frames when flowering is over.

Miniature winter or spring flowering bulbs are often combined with alpines in this programme, and so, too, are dwarf conifers. The latter can also be grown in pans or in pots, and they provide a 'framework' for a display of alpines and bulbs under glass. They can be taken into the cold greenhouse in the autumn and returned to the frames in spring.

Of course, it is necessary to choose only the smallest conifers for this purpose, as some of the dwarfs would really grow too tall eventually for greenhouse display. Those I recommend are *Abies balsamea* 'Hudsonia', *Chamaecyparis lawsoniana* 'Pygmy', *Juniperus communis* 'Compressa', *Picea abies* 'Gregoryana', *Picea abies* 'Nidiformis', *Picea glauca* 'Albertiana Conica', *Picea mariana* 'Nana' and *Pinus mugo* 'Gnom' and 'Mops'.

In order to display alpines and dwarf conifers effectively in a cold greenhouse, I recommend constructing a deep bench, sufficiently strong to hold pea shingle or sand in which to plunge the pots and pans to their rims to hide them. This also prevents rapid drying out of the compost. First, a selection of dwarf conifers should be arranged on the bench, to provide the 'framework' of the display. Then pans of alpines and dwarf bulbs can be arranged around and between them. To complete the picture, a few small pieces of well-shaped rock, in sandstone or limestone, could be partially sunk in the shingle or sand. Such a display needs minimum attention in winter but do open all the ventilators daily to ensure really fresh conditions, except during periods of really severe frost or fog or in snow-storms.

In a cold greenhouse it is possible to use heathers for winter colour, perhaps combining them with the alpines and conifers. Ideal for this purpose are varieties of the winter-flowering heather, *Erica herbacea (E. carnea)*. These could be grown permanently in pots or pans, taken into the greenhouse only when in flower, and returned to the cold frames once the display is over. Although they grow well enough in chalky or limy soils, I prefer to use an acid compost.

Potted heathers could also be taken indoors to provide colour in a cool room. Stand them on a windowsill in maximum light, but do not keep them indoors for longer than a week at a time, or growth may become weak and etiolated.

Below Dwarf conifers in pots and pans make excellent companions for alpines and miniature bulbs in a cold greenhouse

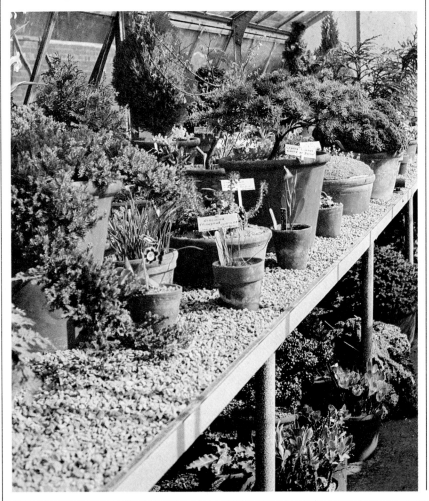

Growing a Christmas Tree

This book would not be complete without mention of Christmas trees for, of course, these are conifers. The traditional Christmas tree (that is, in the U.K.), is the Norway spruce, *Picea abies*. These are grown in their thousands for sale at Christmas time.

There are other conifers, however, that may appeal to you for use as Christmas trees. They are not too different in appearance from the Norway spruce and include the noble fir, *Abies procera*, which is highly popular in Denmark as a Christmas tree; the grand fir, *Abies grandis*; and the Douglas fir, *Pseudotsuga menziesii*.

If you want to keep a Christmas tree from year to year it is no good buying one from a market stall or greengrocer, for even though it may have roots, it will not survive. The roots will have been badly damaged during lifting and they will have completely dried out. Any fibrous roots still attached will have died.

Instead, buy a tree from a tree and shrub nurseryman or garden centre: one that is well established in a pot. Such trees should be of good quality — a rich, deep shade of green, and have a regular pyramidal shape. They should be broad at the base, gradually tapering to the top, and have a bushy or well-branched habit.

The tree can be transferred to an ornamental tub of suitable size when you get it home. The tub should be slightly wider than the rootball. Details of planting in containers will be found in Chapter Five. Do make sure that the tub has drainage holes in the bottom. I rather like wooden tubs for Christmas trees.

The tree should be grown permanently in a tub for best results. Planting it in the garden each year after the festive season, and then lifting it again and potting will check its growth, and there is always the possibility that it will die. However, if you decide to keep a tree in a tub, from year to year, bear in mind that the compost must not be allowed to dry out at any time as this will cause needle drop. You must keep a close eye on water requirements, particularly during warm, dry weather in the spring and summer. I suggest that the container is plunged to its rim in the soil to prevent rapid drying out. Choose an open, sunny part of the garden in which to keep the tree.

A Christmas tree should be left outside until as near Christmas day as possible, for the less time it spends indoors the better. Before taking the tree indoors, I suggest spraying it with a proprietary anti-transpirant spray, sold in aerosol form. This will prevent it from losing moisture rapidly through its leaves, which can result in needle drop.

Of course, the tree will detest a hot stuffy room with a dry atmosphere: indeed, such conditions will do it no good at all. Instead, put it in the coolest possible room and set it close to a window for maximum light. An ideal place, perhaps, would be an unheated hallway if there is adequate light. An unheated, enclosed porch would also be suitable, provided that there is sufficient space. The tree would provide a pleasant welcome for visitors. Do not forget to keep it watered while it is indoors.

As soon as Twelfth Night arrives — the end of the festive season — return the tree to the garden, giving it another anti-transpirant spray.

A Christmas tree, if happy, should make about 30cm (12in) of growth per year, so if you start off with a small tree — say, in the region of 1m (3ft) high — it should give a good few years' service. Eventually, of course, it will become too large to take indoors. Then you will have to make a decision. Do you plant it in the garden or discard it? All I would say is that Christmas trees, of whatever type, eventually develop into huge specimens, suitable only for very large gardens. For instance, the ultimate height of *Picea abies* is 30–40m (100–132ft), with a spread of about 10m (33ft).

Above Picea abies, the Norway spruce or Christmas tree, can be kept for many years if it is carefully looked after

Below The new spring growth of *Picea abies* is most attractive. This tree is capable of making about 30cm (12in) of growth in a year when happy

CHAPTER SIX

ORNAMENTAL CONIFERS

Opposite All shades of green are to be found in conifers, and there are grey, blue and golden kinds. For best foliage colour grow them in an open, sunny position

Right Abies balsamea 'Hudsonia' is very slow growing and ideal for rock gardens and containers. Here it's growing with aubrieta

THERE ARE HUNDREDS of conifers available when all the species and varieties of the major genera are taken into account. However, in this chapter I have not simply catalogued them, but have carefully selected those which I consider are among the very best for gardens. Here are conifers for the smallest plot (even a sink garden) to the largest garden — something to suit every requirement. For ease of reference I have grouped them under their well-known common names, such as the firs, cedars, Lawson cypresses, junipers, spruces, pines, yews, and so on.

The Firs

Abies balsamea 'Hudsonia'
SILVER FIR

SHAPE Very compact, dense, bun shaped.

SIZE Very slow growing, attaining about 30cm (12in) in height in 10 years, but ultimately about 1m high by 1.2m across (3 by 4ft).

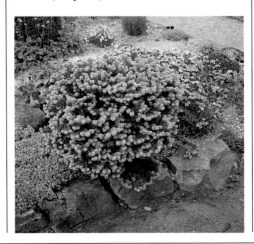

FOLIAGE Evergreen, extremely dense, deep green and shiny. The new spring growth is particularly attractive and a notable feature.

SPECIAL CONDITIONS Very hardy and can be grown anywhere in Britain.

SPECIAL USES 'Hudsonia' is particularly recommended for small rock gardens and would also be suitable for small ornamental containers.

Abies concolor
WHITE FIR

SHAPE Forms an attractive pyramid.

SIZE Large, attaining, after about 20 years 10m in height and 1.8–2.4m across (33 by 6–8ft).

FOLIAGE Evergreen, the greyish green leaves creating a marvellous overall feathery texture. Cones, green and purple, about 12.5cm (5in) long are not often produced. A good point about this conifer is that the lower branches are retained for a long time.

SPECIAL CONDITIONS No particular fads — very adaptable.

SPECIAL USES As a specimen conifer — say, in a lawn, or in a large mixed group.

Abies koreana
KOREAN FIR

SHAPE Forms a pleasing pyramid.

SIZE Large, ultimately attaining a height of 15m with a spread of about 3–3.6m (50 by 10–12ft).

FOLIAGE Evergreen, on top green and shiny, but underneath whitish. Unlike most abies, this species produces cones when it is quite young, which are purple and most attractive.

SPECIAL CONDITIONS Very adaptable with no special requirements.

Right The monkey puzzle, or *Araucaria araucana*, will eventually grow up to 30m (100ft) high and almost as wide

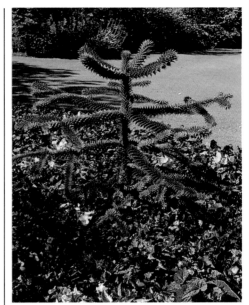

SPECIAL USES Primarily used as a specimen plant, perhaps in a lawn, but also recommended for large mixed groups.

Abies pinsapo
SPANISH FIR

SHAPE A good pyramid, broader than most other abies.

SIZE Large, ultimately attaining about 20–25m in height and about 9m across (66–83 by 30ft).

FOLIAGE Evergreen, deep green and very dense. Cylindrical purple-brown cones are an attractive feature.

SPECIAL CONDITIONS Ideal for growing in chalky soils.

SPECIAL USES Highly recommended as a specimen plant in a large lawn — would create a superb focal point.

Abies procera 'Glauca Prostrata'
DWARF NOBLE FIR

SHAPE A prostrate form of the noble fir.

SIZE Very slow growing, attaining 30cm in height by 1m across (12in by 3ft) in 10 years.

FOLIAGE The evergreen leaves are deep blue-grey, the colour being especially good on the new growth.

SPECIAL CONDITIONS Needs acid or lime-free soil.

SPECIAL USES An excellent conifer for a heather garden, or for a mixed group of dwarf conifers.

The Monkey Puzzle

Araucaria araucana
MONKEY PUZZLE

SHAPE Overall shape a broad dome, but has semi-pendulous branches, the lowest of which can sweep down to the ground.

SIZE Ultimately 25–30m (84–100ft) high, and almost as wide. However, it is a very slow grower and in 10 years from planting will be only about 1.2m (4ft) in height.

FOLIAGE Evergreen, carried in spirals along the branches, deep green, glossy and spine-tipped. Becomes bare at the base as it matures, exposing an attractive, thick trunk.

SPECIAL CONDITIONS Very hardy (comes from Chile and Argentina), grows best in moist soils.

SPECIAL USES As a specimen conifer in a lawn. Was very popular with the Victorians, so a good choice if you have a house of that period.

The Cedars

Cedrus atlantica 'Glauca'
BLUE ATLAS CEDAR

SHAPE Develops into a pyramid.

SIZE A massive conifer only suited to very large gardens and estates. Ultimate height and spread 35–40m by 9–10m (115–132 by 30–33ft).

Below The colour of *Abies procera* 'Glauca Prostrata' is particularly bright on the new growth

FOLIAGE Evergreen, blue-green to grey-green, the colour being particularly intense in winter. Older trees produce most attractive bluish cones.

SPECIAL CONDITIONS Very hardy, but needing well-drained soil. Young trees should be securely staked until well established.

SPECIAL USES As a specimen tree in a large lawn. There is no doubt that this is one of the most beautiful of all large conifers. It grows well in maritime areas.

Cedrus deodara
DEODAR CEDAR

SHAPE Its overall shape is pyramidal, but it has drooping branches.

SIZE A large conifer, at first slow to make growth, but then it accelerates. Ultimate height is 50m with a spread of 10m (165 by 33ft).

FOLIAGE A graceful evergreen, the foliage blue-green when first produced in the spring, turning to deep green as it ages.

SPECIAL CONDITIONS Needs well-drained soil.

SPECIAL USES As a specimen tree in a lawn. Ideal choice for maritime areas.

Cedrus deodara 'Golden Horizon'
GOLDEN DEODAR CEDAR

SHAPE Semi-prostrate in habit with pendulous branches.

SIZE A slow grower, attaining a maximum of 75cm in height, with a spread of 1.2m (2½ by 4ft) in 10 years from planting.

FOLIAGE Evergreen, golden in colour.

SPECIAL CONDITIONS Needs well-drained soil.

SPECIAL USES An excellent choice for planting in a heather garden, or for including in a mixed group of small conifers.

Cedrus libani
CEDAR OF LEBANON

SHAPE Cone-shaped when young but gradually develops into a flat-topped tree.

SIZE Very large, only suited to the largest gardens and estates. Ultimate height and spread 25–40m by 9m (83–132 by 30ft).

FOLIAGE Evergreen, colour variable — bright to deep green; can look sombre. Dark grey bark.

SPECIAL CONDITIONS Best in warm, drier parts of the British Isles.

SPECIAL USES As a specimen tree in a large lawn. Ideal for maritime areas.

The Plum Yew

Cephalotaxus harringtonia drupacea
JAPANESE PLUM YEW

SHAPE Forms a rounded bush.

SIZE Ultimate height and spread 2–3m (6–10ft), but attains about 90cm (3ft) in 10 years.

FOLIAGE Evergreen, like a large-leaved yew, but pale green. Olive-green plum-like fruits are produced.

SPECIAL CONDITIONS Excellent for shade and for chalky soils.

SPECIAL USES Grow as a specimen or in a mixed group. This is an unusual and little-known conifer, but is available from specialist growers and worth growing.

The Lawson Cypresses

Chamaecyparis lawsoniana
LAWSON CYPRESS

SHAPE Used only as a hedging or screening plant.

SIZE Can be clipped to form a suitable-sized hedge — say, 1.8–2.4m (6–8ft) high.

FOLIAGE Evergreen, deepish green, aromatic, dense and carried in flat sprays.

SPECIAL CONDITIONS Very adaptable with no special fads. Do not cut into old wood when pruning.

SPECIAL USES For hedging and screening. The variety 'Green Hedger' has rich green foliage and is a better choice than the species.

Chamaecyparis lawsoniana 'Allumii'
LAWSON CYPRESS

SHAPE Forms a cone-shaped specimen.

SIZE Compact, ultimate height and spread 10–15 by 3m (33–50 by 10ft).

FOLIAGE Evergreen, distinctive bluish grey.

SPECIAL CONDITIONS As C. lawsoniana.

SPECIAL USES Very popular, used as a specimen, in mixed groups, in a heather garden or formal areas, and as hedging.

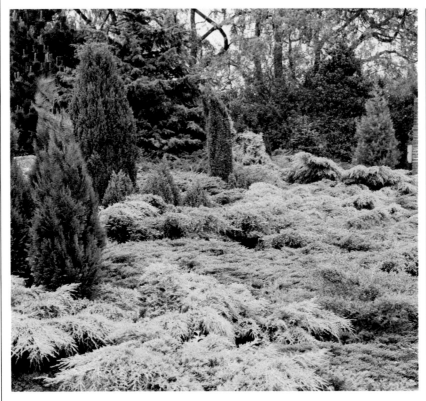

Above This attractive garden includes *Chamaecyparis lawsoniana* 'Allumii' (cone shape), *Juniperus x media* 'Pfitzerana', *J. x media* 'Pfitzerana Aurea', and *Juniperus squamata* 'Meyeri'

Chamaecyparis lawsoniana 'Blue Nantais'
LAWSON CYPRESS

SHAPE Forms a cone-shaped specimen.

SIZE A slow grower, attaining about 1m (3ft) in 10 years.

FOLIAGE Evergreen, silvery blue in summer, turning to greyish green in winter.

SPECIAL CONDITIONS As *C. lawsoniana*.

SPECIAL USES Excellent for heather gardens or beds, and also attractive when included in a mixed group of small conifers.

Chamaecyparis lawsoniana 'Columnaris'
LAWSON CYPRESS

SHAPE Forms a narrow pillar.

SIZE Ultimately attains 7–9m in height with a spread of 2.4–3m (23–30 by 8–10ft).

FOLIAGE Evergreen, bluish grey.

SPECIAL CONDITIONS As *C. lawsoniana*.

SPECIAL USES This is a very popular conifer, being used as a specimen — say, in a lawn or in the heather garden — and excellent when grouped with golden-leaved conifers or heathers.

Chamaecyparis lawsoniana 'Ellwoodii'
LAWSON CYPRESS

SHAPE Forms a very compact cone shape.

SIZE Ultimate size is 4.5–6m in height, with a spread of 1.8–2.4m (15–20 by 6–8ft).

FOLIAGE Evergreen, very dense, grey-green, but becoming bluish in the winter.

SPECIAL CONDITIONS As *C. lawsoniana*.

SPECIAL USES An ideal choice for tubs; can also be planted in rock gardens or in the heather garden; makes a pleasing specimen conifer in the smaller garden.

Chamaecyparis lawsoniana 'Ellwood's Gold'
LAWSON CYPRESS

SHAPE Forms a very compact cone.

SIZE Small, slow-growing, attaining about 1.5m (5ft) in height in 10 years.

FOLIAGE Evergreen, with a soft feathery appearance, flushed with yellow in the summer.

SPECIAL CONDITIONS As *C. lawsoniana*, but it needs sun for the best foliage colour.

SPECIAL USES Ideal for growing in tubs, in a mixed group of small conifers, or as a specimen plant in the heather garden. A first-class conifer — highly recommended.

Chamaecyparis lawsoniana 'Ellwood's Pillar'
LAWSON CYPRESS

SHAPE Forms a very narrow cone.

SIZE Will not attain more than 75cm (2½ft) in 10 years.

FOLIAGE Evergreen, dense and feathery, blue-grey.

SPECIAL CONDITIONS As *C. lawsoniana*.

SPECIAL USES Ideal for the small rock garden and tubs.

Chamaecyparis lawsoniana 'Fletcheri'
LAWSON CYPRESS

SHAPE Forms a broad column, but of very compact habit.

SIZE Ultimately makes a specimen 5–7m in height by 1.8–2.4m in width (16–23 by 6–8ft).

FOLIAGE Evergreen, soft, greyish green in colour.

SPECIAL CONDITIONS As *C. lawsoniana.*

SPECIAL USES Extremely popular, ideal for the smaller garden. It makes a good specimen plant and is an excellent choice for the heather bed. It is also a good hedging conifer.

Chamaecyparis lawsoniana 'Forsteckensis'
LAWSON CYPRESS

SHAPE Very compact, forming a bun shape.

SIZE A very slow grower, attaining only 30cm (12in) in height after 10 years. Ultimately makes a specimen about 1 by 1.5m (3 by 5ft).

FOLIAGE Evergreen, grey-green.

SPECIAL CONDITIONS As *C. lawsoniana.*

SPECIAL USES Ideal for the small rock garden, for ornamental containers and for the heather bed.

Chamaecyparis lawsoniana 'Gnome'
LAWSON CYPRESS

SHAPE Forms a very tiny cone.

SIZE Will attain no more than 30cm (12in) in height in 10 years.

FOLIAGE Evergreen, extremely dense, dark green.

SPECIAL CONDITIONS As *C. lawsoniana.*

SPECIAL USES Ideal for the small rock garden and for small ornamental containers.

Chamaecyparis lawsoniana 'Green Pillar'
LAWSON CYPRESS

SHAPE The branches are erect, forming a columnar shape.

SIZE Ultimate size is 10–12m in height, with a spread of 3m (33–40 by 10ft).

FOLIAGE Evergreen, bright green, with a pleasing texture. The foliage is carried in upright layers.

SPECIAL CONDITIONS As *C. lawsoniana.*

SPECIAL USES Makes a good specimen plant and is also recommended for the heather garden.

Chamaecyparis lawsoniana 'Lanei'
LAWSON CYPRESS

SHAPE Forms a broad cone.

SIZE Ultimate size is 10–15m in height, with a spread of 5m (33–50 by 16ft).

FOLIAGE Evergreen, golden, good colour being maintained all year round, but perhaps even better in winter.

SPECIAL CONDITIONS As *C. lawsoniana,* but needs sunny position for best colour.

SPECIAL USES One of the best of the golden Lawsons, making an attractive specimen plant in a lawn or heather garden. Marvellous in a mixed group when planted near 'blue' conifers. Try it also as a hedge.

Chamaecyparis lawsoniana 'Lutea'
LAWSON CYPRESS

SHAPE Forms a broad cone.

SIZE Ultimate size is 10–12m in height, with a spread of 5m (33–40 by 16ft).

FOLIAGE Evergreen, golden, the colour being particularly bright in the winter.

SPECIAL CONDITIONS As *C. lawsoniana,* but remember that it needs plenty

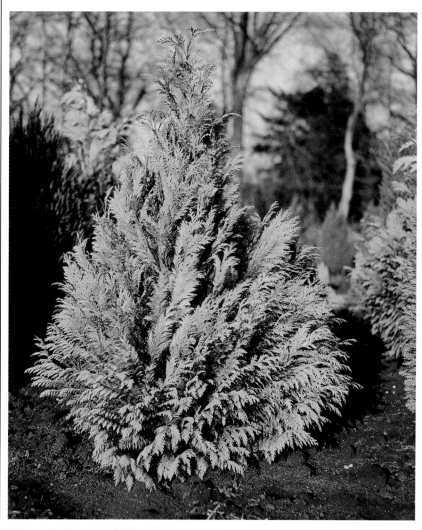

Below Chamaecyparis lawsoniana 'Lanei' is one of the best of the golden Lawsons, but eventually makes quite a large specimen

of sun for the best foliage colour.

SPECIAL USES A very popular golden conifer: same uses as 'Lanei'.

Chamaecyparis lawsoniana 'Minima Aurea'
LAWSON CYPRESS

SHAPE Forms a cone.

SIZE A very slow grower, attaining only 35cm (13in) after 10 years. Ultimately 1.2–1.5m (4–5ft) in height and spread.

FOLIAGE Evergreen, very dense, bright yellow all the year round, but particularly intense in winter.

SPECIAL CONDITIONS As *C. lawsoniana*, but provide a position in full sun.

SPECIAL USES Ideal for a small rock garden, ornamental tubs, or for the heather garden.

Chamaecyparis lawsoniana 'Pembury Blue'
LAWSON CYPRESS

SHAPE Makes a broad cone.

SIZE Ultimately 7–10m in height with a spread of 2.4m (23–33 by 8ft).

FOLIAGE Evergreen, silvery blue — indeed, the 'bluest' of the Lawsons.

SPECIAL CONDITIONS As *C. lawsoniana*.

SPECIAL USES Makes an excellent specimen in a lawn and looks good in a mixed group, particularly if positioned near golden conifers. A good choice, too, for the heather garden.

Chamaecyparis lawsoniana 'Pixie'
LAWSON CYPRESS

SHAPE Forms a neat globe-shaped bush.

SIZE Attains no more than 50 by 50cm (10 by 10in) in 10 years.

FOLIAGE Evergreen, with a soft texture and bluish green in colour.

SPECIAL CONDITIONS As *C. lawsoniana*.

SPECIAL USES An excellent choice for the small rock garden, for ornamental containers such as tubs and window boxes, and for grouping in the heather garden or with other small conifers.

Chamaecyparis lawsoniana 'Pygmy'
LAWSON CYPRESS

SHAPE Develops into a neat globe-shaped bush.

SIZE No more than 30 by 30cm (12 by 12in) in 10 years from planting.

FOLIAGE Evergreen, grey-green and very dense.

SPECIAL CONDITIONS As *C. lawsoniana*.

SPECIAL USES As for *C. l.* 'Pixie'. Also recommended for sink gardens.

Chamaecyparis lawsoniana 'Stewartii'
LAWSON CYPRESS

SHAPE Develops into a broad cone.

SIZE Ultimately 10–14m in height by 4.5m across (33–45 by 15ft).

FOLIAGE Evergreen with narrow sprays of foliage, golden, but turning yellow-green in the winter.

SPECIAL CONDITIONS Needs full sun for the best colour, otherwise as for *C. lawsoniana*.

SPECIAL USES Very popular, used in the same way as *C. l.* 'Lanei'.

Chamaecyparis lawsoniana 'Winston Churchill'
LAWSON CYPRESS

SHAPE Forms a broad cone.

SIZE A slow grower, but ultimately 6–8m in height by 3–4m across (20–27 by 10–13ft).

FOLIAGE Evergreen and dense, rich gold, holding its colour well all the year round.

SPECIAL CONDITIONS Full sun for best colour, otherwise as for *C. lawsoniana*.

SPECIAL USES As for *C. l.* 'Lanei'.

The Nootka Cypress

Chamaecyparis nootkatensis 'Pendula'
NOOTKA CYPRESS

SHAPE The branches turn up at the tips but the branchlets are pendulous. The tree is slow to attain this distinctive habit.

SIZE Ultimately 25m in height by 10m in width (80 by 33ft).

FOLIAGE Evergreen, dullish green with a coarse texture.

SPECIAL CONDITIONS After planting, train the leading shoot to a stake to ensure that it grows straight.

SPECIAL USES Makes a superb and distinctive specimen tree in a lawn, useful on cold sites.

The Hinoki Cypresses

Chamaecyparis obtusa 'Crippsii'
HINOKI CYPRESS

SHAPE Forms a pyramid shape, of loose, open habit.

SIZE Ultimately 8m in height with a spread of 3m (28 by 10ft).

FOLIAGE Deep golden, especially bright in the winter.

SPECIAL CONDITIONS Adaptable, but needs full sun for best colour.

SPECIAL USES As a specimen tree in a lawn, in the heather garden, or in a group with 'blue' conifers.

Chamaecyparis obtusa 'Goldilocks'
HINOKI CYPRESS

SHAPE Forms a broad-based pyramid.

SIZE A slow grower; probable height in 10 years 1.5m (5ft).

FOLIAGE Evergreen, dense, golden-yellow.

SPECIAL CONDITIONS Adaptable, but needs full sun for best colour.

SPECIAL USES Mixed groups of small conifers, or in the heather garden — looks good with greyish-leaved heathers.

Chamaecyparis obtusa 'Nana Gracilis'
HINOKI CYPRESS

SHAPE Forms a bun shape, or a very broad cone.

SIZE Attains a maximum height and spread of 60cm (2ft) in 10 years, but ultimately 4–5m (14–17ft) in height and spread.

FOLIAGE Evergreen, carried in shell-like sprays, deep green and shiny.

SPECIAL CONDITIONS Adaptable, can be grown in shade.

SPECIAL USES Very popular, being ideal for the heather garden, mixed groups of small conifers, in containers or in the small rock garden.

Chamaecyparis obtusa 'Tetragona Aurea'
HINOKI CYPRESS

SHAPE Has no definite shape, but has upswept branches.

SIZE Attains about 90cm (3ft) in 10 years, but ultimately 4–5m (14–17ft) in height and spread.

FOLIAGE Evergreen, in dense tufts, bright golden-yellow.

SPECIAL CONDITIONS Full sun is needed for the best colour.

SPECIAL USES As a specimen plant, in a mixed group or in the heather garden.

The Sawara Cypresses

Chamaecyparis pisifera 'Boulevard'
SAWARA CYPRESS

SHAPE Forms a broad cone.

SIZE Attains about 1.2m (4ft) in 10 years; ultimately 3–4m (10–13ft) in height and spread.

FOLIAGE Evergreen, silvery blue, especially colourful in the summer.

SPECIAL CONDITIONS Needs moist soil, so avoid dry conditions. Lime and clay soils are not suitable, either. Relishes humid air.

SPECIAL USES Very popular, it looks good in a mixed group of small conifers or in the heather garden.

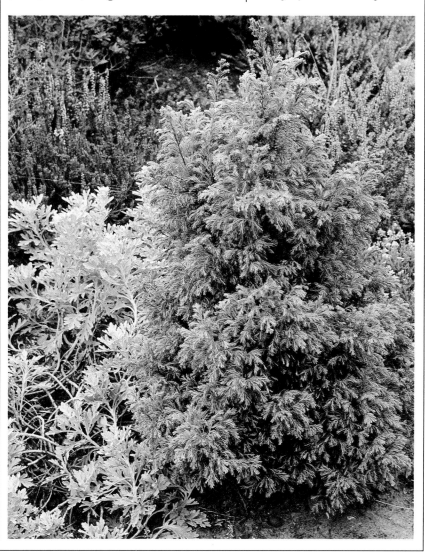

Below Chamaecyparis pisifera 'Boulevard' is one of the most popular dwarf conifers and looks good in a mixed group or in a heather garden

Chamaecyparis pisifera 'Filifera Aurea'
SAWARA CYPRESS

SHAPE Dome-shaped, with weeping branchlets.
SIZE Attains about 1.2m in height and spread after 10 years; ultimately 3–5m (10–16ft) in height and spread.
FOLIAGE Evergreen, thread-like, and bright yellow all the year round.
SPECIAL CONDITIONS As for *C. p.* 'Boulevard', but needs full sun for best colour.
SPECIAL USES As for *C. p.* 'Boulevard'.

Chamaecyparis pisifera 'Gold Spangle'
SAWARA CYPRESS

SHAPE Forms a dome shape.
SIZE After 10 years about 90 by 60cm (3 by 2ft) in height and spread.
FOLIAGE Evergreen, loose, open, brilliant gold, giving excellent winter colour.
SPECIAL CONDITIONS As for *C. p.* 'Boulevard', but needs full sun for best colour.
SPECIAL USES Heather garden or mixed groups of small conifers.

Chamaecyparis pisifera 'Plumosa Aurea Nana'
SAWARA CYPRESS

SHAPE Forms a broad cone.
SIZE Ultimately 1–1.5m (3–5ft) in height and spread, but only 60cm (2ft) after 10 years.
FOLIAGE Evergreen, beautiful texture (soft and feathery), bright yellow, the colour being particularly good in winter.
SPECIAL CONDITIONS As for *C. p.* 'Boulevard'; provide full sun for really good foliage colour.
SPECIAL USES As for *C. p.* 'Boulevard'; also recommended for tubs.

Chamaecyparis pisifera 'Squarrosa sulphurea'
SAWARA CYPRESS

SHAPE Forms a globe-shaped bush.
SIZE In 10 years it will attain about 1m in height, with a spread of 75cm (3 by 2½ft).
FOLIAGE Evergreen, in summer bright sulphur yellow.
SPECIAL CONDITIONS As for *C. p.* 'Boulevard', but ensure plenty of sun.
SPECIAL USES Particularly recommended for a heather garden, or mixed group of small conifers.

The White Cypresses

Chamaecyparis thyoides 'Andelyensis'
WHITE CYPRESS

SHAPE Narrow cone or column.
SIZE A very slow grower; about 1m (3ft) in height after 10 years; ultimately 5 by 1.5m in height and spread (17 by 5ft).
FOLIAGE Evergreen, blue-green, turning bronzy in the winter.
SPECIAL CONDITIONS Best on moist soils; avoid chalky conditions.
SPECIAL USES Ideal for containers; also for the heather garden and mixed groups of small conifers.

Chamaecyparis thyoides 'Ericoides'
WHITE CYPRESS

SHAPE Bun shaped.
SIZE About 60cm (2ft) in height and spread after 10 years; ultimately 1–1.5m (3–5ft) in height, with a similar spread.
FOLIAGE Evergreen, bronze-green in summer, changing to purple in winter.

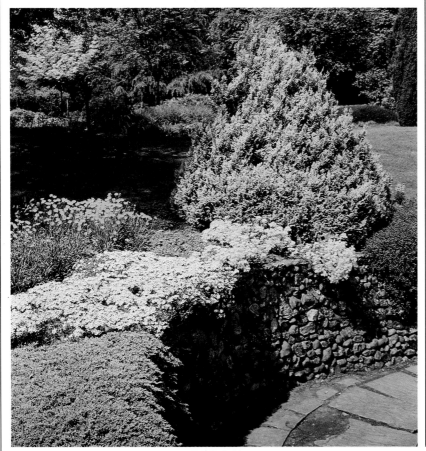

Below Chamaecyparis pisifera 'Plumosa Aurea Nana' growing with alyssum, alpine phlox and *Juniperus procumbens* 'Nana' (foreground)

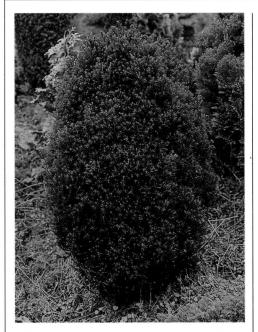

SPECIAL CONDITIONS As for *C. t.* 'Andelyensis'. Prone to winter weather damage, so choose a sheltered spot.

SPECIAL USES Looks particularly good when grown with red-flowered winter heathers. Also useful in ornamental containers or in mixed groups of small conifers.

The Japanese Cedars

Cryptomeria japonica 'Elegans'
JAPANESE CEDAR

SHAPE Broad cone shape.

SIZE About 2m (6ft) in height after 10 years; ultimately 6–8m in height with a spread of 3.6–4.8m (20–27 by 12–16ft).

FOLIAGE Evergreen, soft and feathery, brownish green in summer, turning reddish bronze in the winter.

SPECIAL CONDITIONS Needs a sunny sheltered spot. Will take some shade, but growth and colour may not be quite so good. Requires slightly acid, moist but well-drained soil.

SPECIAL USES Excellent as a specimen conifer; or can be used in a mixed group of medium-sized conifers — try associating it with grey-leaved kinds.

Cryptomeria japonica 'Sekkan Sugi'
JAPANESE CEDAR

SHAPE Dome shaped.

SIZE A very slow grower: maximum height after 10 years 2m (6ft).

FOLIAGE Evergreen, in early summer

the young leaves are creamy white, while in winter they are cream, lightly flushed with bronze.

SPECIAL CONDITIONS As for *C. j.* 'Elegans', but provide a position in full sun, and protect the plant from cold winds and hard frosts.

SPECIAL USES Heather garden, or mixed groups of small conifers. Looks particularly good with pink heathers.

Cryptomeria japonica 'Vilmoriniana'
JAPANESE CEDAR

SHAPE Bun shaped and very compact.

SIZE 30cm (12in) in height after 10 years; ultimately 1m (3ft) in height and spread.

FOLIAGE Evergreen, dense, bright green, turning deep reddish purple in winter.

SPECIAL CONDITIONS As for *C. j.* 'Elegans'; will take some shade.

SPECIAL USES Very popular, ideal for the small rock garden, heather garden or containers. Try it with red or pink winter-flowering heathers.

Left Chamaecyparis thyoides 'Ericoides' is bronze-green in summer, changing to purple in the winter. It's a dwarf grower

Below The winter colour of *Cryptomeria japonica* 'Elegans' with a background of variegated ivy

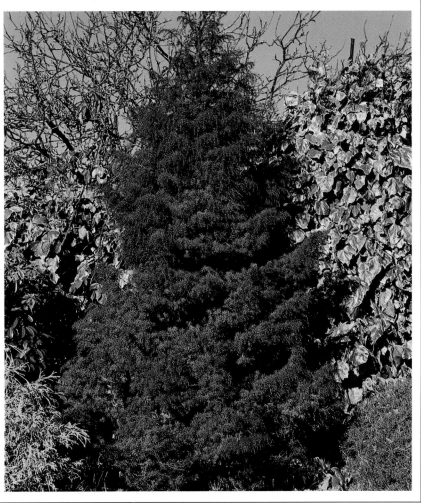

Right A young hedge of x *Cupressocyparis* leylandii 'Castlewellan', ideal for coastal gardens

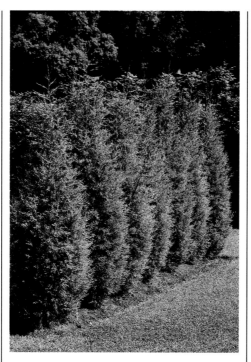

Below The maidenhair tree, or *Ginkgo biloba*, will ultimately attain at least 20m (66ft) and is essentially a specimen tree

The Leyland Cypress

x *Cupressocyparis leylandii*
LEYLAND CYPRESS

SHAPE Broad cone shape.

SIZE A rapid grower, putting on up to 1m (3ft) of growth in a year. Ultimately 25–30m in height by 4.8m in width (82–100 by 16ft).

FOLIAGE Evergreen, variable in colour, the typical colour being greyish green. There is also a pale yellow form called 'Castlewellan' which is becoming popular.

SPECIAL CONDITIONS Adaptable, but ideal for coastal gardens. It is best to provide a stake for newly planted trees, until they are well rooted in the soil.

SPECIAL USES Used for hedging, screens and windbreaks.

The Monterey Cypresses

Cupressus macrocarpa
MONTEREY CYPRESS

SHAPE Cone shaped.

SIZE Ultimately 20m in height with a spread of 6m (68 by 20ft).

FOLIAGE Evergreen, bright green.

SPECIAL CONDITIONS A severe winter can kill plants in very cold parts of the country. Foliage can be browned or scorched by cold drying winds. Most successful in mild coastal areas. Stake young plants until they are well established.

SPECIAL USES Hedges and screens, especially in coastal areas.

Cupressus macrocarpa 'Goldcrest'
MONTEREY CYPRESS

SHAPE Cone shaped.

SIZE Ultimately 10m in height with a spread of 3m (33 by 10ft).

FOLIAGE Evergreen, brilliant golden yellow, which stands out particularly well in winter.

SPECIAL CONDITIONS As for *C. macrocarpa*. Provide a position in full sun for best foliage colour.

SPECIAL USES Generally planted as a specimen — say, in a lawn. Also looks good in a group, near to grey or 'blue' conifers. Makes a good hedge or screen, particularly in coastal areas.

The Maidenhair Tree

Ginkgo biloba
MAIDENHAIR TREE

SHAPE Roughly pyramid shaped.

SIZE Slow to become established, but ultimate height is at least 20m with a spread of 6m (66 by 20ft).

FOLIAGE Deciduous, fan-shaped light green leaves which turn deep yellow in autumn before they fall.

SPECIAL CONDITIONS Likes a sheltered sunny spot, thriving in any ordinary garden soil containing plenty of humus.

SPECIAL USES Essentially a specimen tree for a lawn.

The Junipers

Juniperus chinensis 'Japonica'
CHINESE JUNIPER

SHAPE A roughly rounded bush with pendulous shoot tips.

SIZE About 60cm (2ft) high after 10 years; ultimately 1.5–2m high and 2–2.5m across (5–6 by 6–8ft).

FOLIAGE Evergreen, deceptively soft looking but very prickly; light green.

SPECIAL CONDITIONS Ideal for chalky soils; tolerates drought extremely well.

SPECIAL USES Often planted in rock gardens; ideal, too, for the heather garden or mixed groups.

Juniperus chinensis 'Kuriwao Gold'
CHINESE JUNIPER

SHAPE Globular or dome shaped.

SIZE In 10 years attains no more than 1.5m in height with a spread of 1m (5 by 3ft).

FOLIAGE Evergreen, very dense, yellow-green all the year round.

SPECIAL CONDITIONS As for *J. chinensis* 'Japonica'; very hardy.

SPECIAL USES Mixed groups of small conifers, or heather garden.

Juniperus chinensis 'Pyramidalis'
CHINESE JUNIPER

SHAPE Broad cone shape.

SIZE About 2m (6ft) in height after 10 years; ultimately 3–4m (10–14ft), the spread being about two-thirds of the height.

FOLIAGE Evergreen, prickly, greyish or bluish green.

SPECIAL CONDITIONS As for *J. chinensis* 'Japonica'.

SPECIAL USES Looks good in the heather garden surrounded by pink-flowered heathers.

Juniperus communis 'Compressa'
VARIETY OF COMMON JUNIPER

SHAPE Very narrow column.

SIZE Ultimate height 1m (3ft), but extremely slow growing, attaining about 30–45cm (12–18in) after 10 years. Spread about 15cm (6in).

FOLIAGE Evergreen, very dense and prickly, grey-green.

SPECIAL CONDITIONS Grows well in chalky soils and likes full sun.

SPECIAL USES There is probably no better conifer for sink gardens, small containers and tiny rock gardens. Grow it on its own, or in a group of three plants.

Juniperus communis 'Depressa Aurea'
VARIETY OF COMMON JUNIPER

SHAPE Prostrate — forms a mat.

SIZE spreads ultimately to 4m (14ft); 1–1.5m (3–5ft) in 10 years.

FOLIAGE Evergreen, golden-yellow in summer, bronze in winter; and very prickly.

SPECIAL CONDITIONS As for *J. communis* 'Compressa'.

SPECIAL USES Excellent for ground cover, e.g. for sunny banks.

Juniperus communis 'Green Carpet'
VARIETY OF COMMON JUNIPER

SHAPE Prostrate — forms a dense mat.

SIZE A slow grower, in 10 years attaining 15cm (6in) in height with a spread of 90cm (3ft).

FOLIAGE Evergreen, extremely dense, deep green but becoming bright green in the summer.

SPECIAL CONDITIONS As for *J. communis* 'Compressa'.

SPECIAL USES Ideal for ground cover; also recommended as a specimen in a rock garden, or for trailing over low walls.

Juniperus communis 'Hibernica'
IRISH JUNIPER

SHAPE Fastigiate — forms a very narrow column.

SIZE Attains a height of about 2m (6ft) in 10 years; ultimately 4.5–6m high (15–20ft).

FOLIAGE Evergreen, very prickly, grey-green.

SPECIAL CONDITIONS As for *J. communis* 'Compressa'.

SPECIAL USES Ideal for use as a focal point in formal areas, as a specimen plant in a lawn, or in the heather garden.

Juniperus communis 'Repanda'
VARIETY OF COMMON JUNIPER

SHAPE Prostrate — forms a mat.

SIZE Ultimate spread 3m (10ft); 1–1.5m (3–5ft) in 10 years.

FOLIAGE Evergreen, very dense, in thick mats, dullish green, flushed with bronze in winter.

SPECIAL CONDITIONS As for *J. communis* 'Compressa'.

SPECIAL USES Ground cover, ideally mixed with ground-cover junipers in other colours.

Juniperus communis 'Suecica Aurea'
VARIETY OF COMMON JUNIPER

SHAPE Forms a narrow column.

SIZE A slow grower, attaining in 10 years only about 1.2m (4ft).

FOLIAGE Evergreen, golden-yellow all the year round.

SPECIAL CONDITIONS As for *J. communis* 'Compressa'.

SPECIAL USES Ideal specimen plant in the small rock garden.

Above For a very bright specimen tree consider *Cupressus macrocarpa* 'Goldcrest', a tall grower

Juniperus conferta
SHORE JUNIPER

SHAPE Prostrate, forms a dense mat.
SIZE Ultimate spread 4m (14ft); 2m (6ft) in 10 years.
FOLIAGE Evergreen, extremely prickly, to the point of being painful if touched. Bright green, excellent texture.
SPECIAL CONDITIONS As for *J. communis* 'Compressa'.
SPECIAL USES Excellent ground cover, and for trailing over low walls or steps.

Juniperus conferta 'Blue Pacific'
SHORE JUNIPER

SHAPE Prostrate, forms a dense mat.
SIZE Slower growing than the species, maximum spread in 10 years about 1.5m (5ft).
FOLIAGE Evergreen, light blue-green.
SPECIAL CONDITIONS As for *J. communis* 'Compressa'.
SPECIAL USES As for *J. conferta*.

Juniperus horizontalis 'Banff'
CREEPING JUNIPER

SHAPE Prostrate — forms a carpet.
SIZE Not too vigorous, maximum spread in 10 years 1m (3ft).
FOLIAGE Evergreen, feathery, pleasing overall texture. Bright silver-blue, best colour in summer.
SPECIAL CONDITIONS Sun-loving and ideal for chalky soils.
SPECIAL USES Essentially a ground-cover plant.

Juniperus horizontalis 'Bar Harbor'
CREEPING JUNIPER

SHAPE Prostrate — forms a mat.
SIZE Ultimate spread 4m (14ft); up to 2m (6ft) in 10 years.
FOLIAGE Evergreen, greyish blue in summer, mauve tinted in winter.
SPECIAL CONDITIONS As for *J. horizontalis* 'Banff'.
SPECIAL USES Ground cover.

Juniperus horizontalis 'Blue Chip'
CREEPING JUNIPER

SHAPE Prostrate — forms a mat.
SIZE Spread in 10 years about 1.5m (5ft).
FOLIAGE Evergreen, feathery, creating a marvellous overall texture. Brilliant silver-blue in summer, but in winter bluish grey.
SPECIAL CONDITIONS As for *J. horizontalis* 'Banff'.
SPECIAL USES Ground cover.

Juniperus horizontalis 'Emerald spreader'
CREEPING JUNIPER

SHAPE Prostrate, very flat.
SIZE Maximum spread in 10 years 2m (6ft)
FOLIAGE Evergreen, emerald green.
SPECIAL CONDITIONS As for *J. horizontalis* 'Banff'.
SPECIAL USES Ground cover.

Juniperus horizontalis 'Glauca'
CREEPING JUNIPER

SHAPE Prostrate — forms a mat.
SIZE Spreads 2–3m (6–10ft) in 10 years; ultimate spread 4m (14ft).
FOLIAGE Evergreen, dense, grey-blue, best colour in summer.
SPECIAL CONDITIONS As for *J. horizontalis* 'Banff'.
SPECIAL USES Ground cover.

Juniperus horizontalis 'Hughes'
CREEPING JUNIPER

SHAPE Prostrate, branches are slightly arching.
SIZE Spread in 10 years 1.5–2m (5–6ft).
FOLIAGE Evergreen, bright silver, with a pleasing overall texure.
SPECIAL CONDITIONS As for *J. horizontalis* 'Banff'.
SPECIAL USES Ground cover. Also makes a pleasing contrast in a mixed group, and looks superb with heathers, especially pink-flowered varieties, or those with golden foliage.

Juniperus horizontalis 'Turquoise Spreader'
CREEPING JUNIPER

SHAPE Prostrate, branches spread widely.
SIZE A slow grower; maximum spread in 10 years 1.2m (4ft).
FOLIAGE Evergreen, very dense, soft and feathery, an unusual shade of turquoise-green.
SPECIAL CONDITIONS As for *J. horizontalis* 'Banff'.
SPECIAL USES A beautiful effect is created if this is planted among golden heathers.

Juniperus x *media* 'Gold Sovereign'
A HYBRID JUNIPER

SHAPE Flat, forms layers of branches.

SIZE Estimated maximum size after 10 years 50cm high and 75cm wide (20in by 2½ft).

FOLIAGE Evergreen, very bright yellow all the year round.

SPECIAL CONDITIONS Needs full sun for best colour; excellent on chalky soils.

SPECIAL USES One of the latest junipers from Bressingham Gardens nursery; a sport of *J.* x *media* 'Old Gold', but growing at half the rate. Use as ground cover, in the heather garden, or in a mixed group of small conifers.

Juniperus x *media* 'Hetzii'
A HYBRID JUNIPER

SHAPE Forms tiers or layers of almost horizontal branches, flattish habit.

SIZE Growing to 1m high by 2m wide (3 by 6ft) in 10 years; ultimately 3 by 4m (10 by 14ft).

FOLIAGE Evergreen, feathery looking overall texture, grey-green.

SPECIAL CONDITIONS Excellent on chalky soil, will grow in shade.

SPECIAL USES Ground cover, heather garden, mixed group of small conifers.

Juniperus x *media* 'Old Gold'
A HYBRID JUNIPER

SHAPE Forms tiers or layers of horizontal branches, the overall shape being flat.

SIZE Growing to 1 by 1m (3 by 3ft) after 10 years; ultimately 2 by 2m (6 by 6ft).

FOLIAGE Evergreen, green-gold all the year round.

SPECIAL CONDITIONS Ideal for chalky soils, needs full sun.

SPECIAL USES Ground cover, heather garden, mixed group of small conifers.

Below Juniperus x *media* 'Old Gold', seen here as a specimen, ultimately attains a height and spread of 2m (6ft)

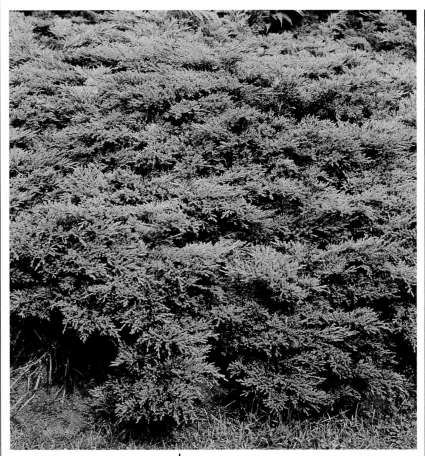

Above Juniperus sabina 'Tamariscifolia' is an excellent ground-cover plant growing no more than 50cm (20in) in height. Spread is 3m (10ft)

Juniperus x *media* 'Pfitzerana Aurea'
GOLDEN PFITZER JUNIPER

SHAPE Flat habit, forms layers of horizontal branches.
SIZE In 10 years reaching 75cm high and 1.5m wide (2½ by 5ft); ultimately 1 by 3m (3 by 10ft).
FOLIAGE Evergreen, golden in summer, yellowish green in winter.
SPECIAL CONDITIONS Needs full sun for best colour, and thrives in chalky soils.
SPECIAL USES Use as ground cover, as a specimen plant, or in a mixed group of small conifers.

Juniperus procumbens 'Nana'
JUNIPER

SHAPE Prostrate, forms a dense mat.
SIZE Ultimately 15cm (6in) high, with a spread of 3m (10ft); spread up to 2m (6ft) in 10 years.
FOLIAGE Evergreen, creating a marvellous textured effect when mass planted, the colour being bright green.
SPECIAL CONDITIONS Excellent on chalky soils.
SPECIAL USES Ground cover.

Juniperus sabina 'Buffalo'
SAVIN JUNIPER

SHAPE Prostrate — forms a low mat.
SIZE Maximum spread in 10 years 1.5m (5ft).
FOLIAGE Evergreen, bright green.
SPECIAL CONDITIONS Ideal for chalk, tolerates shade.
SPECIAL USES Ground cover.

Juniperus sabina 'Tamariscifolia'
SAVIN JUNIPER

SHAPE Prostrate — forms a low mat.
SIZE Growing to 20cm (8in) high and 1m (3ft) across in 10 years; ultimately 50cm by 3m (20in by 10ft).
FOLIAGE Evergreen, feathery, grey-blue.
SPECIAL CONDITIONS As for *J. s.* 'Buffalo'.
SPECIAL USES Ground cover; also looks good when draped over a low wall.

Juniperus scopulorum 'Blue Heaven'
ROCKY MOUNTAIN JUNIPER

SHAPE Forms a pyramid.
SIZE Height in 10 years 2.4m (8ft).
FOLIAGE Evergreen, bright silver-blue, very intense in summer.
SPECIAL CONDITIONS Full sun, ideal for chalk soils.
SPECIAL USES Specimen plant, mixed group, or heather garden.

Juniperus squamata 'Blue Carpet'
JUNIPER

SHAPE Low, but not prostrate, forms a sheet of growth.
SIZE Growing to 30cm high by 2m wide (1 by 6ft) in 10 years.
FOLIAGE Evergreen, brilliant silver-blue.
SPECIAL CONDITIONS Thrives on chalk.
SPECIAL USES Ground cover.

Juniperus squamata 'Blue Star'
JUNIPER

SHAPE Bun shaped.
SIZE Growing to 30 by 50cm (12 by 20in) in 10 years; ultimately 1 by 1m (3 by 3ft).
FOLIAGE Evergreen, prickly, steel blue.
SPECIAL CONDITIONS Ideal for chalky soils.

SPECIAL USES Contrasts well with heathers. Use also in ornamental containers.

Juniperus squamata 'Meyeri'
JUNIPER

SHAPE Distinctive — branches held out at a 45-degree angle.
SIZE Ultimately 3 by 3m (10 by 10ft); about half this in 10 years.
FOLIAGE Evergreen, very hard and prickly, steel blue.
SPECIAL CONDITIONS Ideal for chalky soils. Prune back regularly to keep attractive.
SPECIAL USES As a specimen plant, or in a group of mixed conifers.

Juniperus virginiana 'Grey Owl'
JUNIPER

SHAPE Semi-prostrate.
SIZE A strong grower, attaining about 60cm in height and 2m across (2 by 6ft) in 10 years.
FOLIAGE Evergreen, with greyish tints.
SPECIAL CONDITIONS Ideal for chalky soils.
SPECIAL USES Ground cover.

Juniperus virginiana 'Skyrocket'
JUNIPER

SHAPE Forms a very narrow column.
SIZE Attains about 2m (6ft) in height in

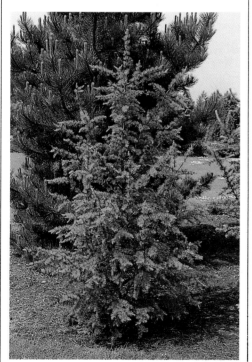

10 years; ultimate height 6–7m (20–23ft).
FOLIAGE Evergreen, bluish grey.
SPECIAL CONDITIONS Grows well in chalky soils.
SPECIAL USES As a specimen plant in, say, a lawn, ideal for a mixed group, or to give height in the heather garden.

The Larch

Larix decidua
EUROPEAN LARCH

SHAPE Roughly cone shaped.
SIZE Ultimately 25–30m in height with a spread of 10m (83–100 by 33ft).
FOLIAGE Deciduous, bright green in spring, turning gold in autumn before it falls.
SPECIAL CONDITIONS Needs an open, sunny position; tolerates windy sites; not suitable for chalky soils.
SPECIAL USES Mainly for screening.

The Dawn Redwood

Metasequoia glyptostroboides
DAWN REDWOOD

SHAPE Roughly cone shaped.
SIZE Ultimately 30–35m (100–115ft) in height with a spread of one-third of this.
FOLIAGE Deciduous, feathery, bright green, turning golden-brown in autumn before it falls. The red-brown bark is very attractive.
SPECIAL CONDITIONS Needs moist soil.
SPECIAL USES As a specimen tree in a lawn.

The Spruces

Picea abies
NORWAY SPRUCE (Christmas tree)

SHAPE Forms a broad cone.
SIZE Ultimately 30–40m high by 10m across (100–132 by 33ft).
FOLIAGE Evergreen, deep green.
SPECIAL CONDITIONS Adaptable, grows well enough on chalk soils.
SPECIAL USES Makes a good screen; not of great ornamental value, apart from its use as a Christmas tree.

Picea abies 'Gregoryana'
DWARF SPRUCE

SHAPE Forms a bun shape.

Above The dawn redwood, *Metasequoia glyptostroboides*, makes a fine specimen tree in a lawn

Left Although it makes an attractive large specimen, the European larch, *Larix decidua*, is mainly used to create tall screens and windbreaks

Above The golden pfitzer juniper, *Juniperus* x *media* 'Pfitzerana Aurea', is golden in summer but turns yellowish green in the winter

SIZE Reaches only 20cm (8in) high in 10 years; ultimately 60cm high by 1.5m wide (2 by 5ft).

FOLIAGE Evergreen, very dense and prickly, greyish green.

SPECIAL CONDITIONS As for *P. abies*.

SPECIAL USES Ideal spruce for the small rock garden, or heather garden.

Picea abies 'Nidiformis'
DWARF SPRUCE

SHAPE Forms a bun shape.

SIZE Growing to 30cm high by 45cm across (12 by 18in) in 10 years; ultimately 1–2 by 2m (3–6 by 6ft).

FOLIAGE Dark green, best colour early summer.

SPECIAL CONDITIONS As for *P. abies*.

SPECIAL USES Small rock garden, containers or heather garden.

Picea brewerana
BREWER'S WEEPING SPRUCE

SHAPE Beautiful pendulous habit, with long drooping branchlets.

SIZE Ultimately 15–20m in height by 5–6m (50–65 by 17–20ft).

FOLIAGE Evergreen, deep bluish green.

SPECIAL CONDITIONS Best results in acid soil and high rainfall areas, sun or shade, sheltered aspect.

SPECIAL USES As a specimen tree in a lawn; not really effective until well established and semi-mature.

Picea glauca 'Albertiana Conica'
WHITE OR CANADIAN SPRUCE

SHAPE Forms a broad cone with soft, bright green foliage.

SIZE About 1m (3ft) high after 10 years; ultimately 2–3m (6–10ft) with a spread of about one-half this.

FOLIAGE Evergreen, very dense, bright green.

SPECIAL CONDITIONS Very adaptable, no particular requirements.

SPECIAL USES Very popular, ideal for the small rock garden, containers and the heather bed.

Picea mariana 'Nana'
DWARF BLACK SPRUCE

SHAPE Bun or ball shaped.

SIZE A very slow grower, at the most 20 by 30cm (8 by 12in) in 10 years.

FOLIAGE Evergreen, very dense, grey-blue, best colour in summer when it is quite bluish.

SPECIAL CONDITIONS Very hardy and adaptable.

SPECIAL USES Ideal for the small rock garden, troughs, sink gardens and for alpine houses.

Picea omorika
SERBIAN SPRUCE

SHAPE Forms a narrow column; the branches turn upwards at the tips.

SIZE Ultimate height 20–25m (66–82ft), with a spread of about one-third of this.

FOLIAGE Evergreen, deep green, grey-green below.

SPECIAL CONDITIONS Takes pollution well, and grows in chalky and dry soils.

SPECIAL USES A superb specimen tree for a lawn; can also be used as a windbreak.

Picea pungens 'Globosa'
A FORM OF THE COLORADO SPRUCE

SHAPE Bun or dome shaped, dense and bushy.

SIZE A slow grower; 60 by 60cm (2 by 2ft) in 10 years; ultimate height and spread 1 by 1m (3 by 3ft).

FOLIAGE Evergreen, brilliant silver-blue, best colour in spring and early summer.

SPECIAL CONDITIONS No particular needs — hardy and adaptable.

SPECIAL USES Looks superb in a

heather bed; gives contrast in a mixed group; can be used as a specimen in the rock garden.

Picea pungens 'Koster'
KOSTER'S BLUE SPRUCE

SHAPE Broad cone.

SIZE Ultimately 7–10m (23–33ft) in height, with a spread of about one-third of this.

FOLIAGE Evergreen, superb silvery blue all the year round — excellent for winter colour.

SPECIAL CONDITIONS No particular needs — hardy and adaptable.

SPECIAL USES Generally used as a specimen in a lawn, but provides contrast in mixed groups.

Picea pungens 'Moerheimii'
A FORM OF THE COLORADO SPRUCE

SHAPE Broad cone.

SIZE Ultimately 7–10m (23–33ft) in height, with a spread of about one-third of this.

FOLIAGE Evergreen, blue-grey, superb for winter colour in the garden.

SPECIAL CONDITIONS No particular needs — hardy and adaptable.

SPECIAL USES As for 'Koster'.

The Pines

Pinus leucodermis 'Compact Gem'
A FORM OF THE BOSNIAN PINE

SHAPE Forms a broad dome.

SIZE A slow grower, eventually attaining about 2 by 2m (6 by 6ft).

FOLIAGE Evergreen, dense, long upright needles, very deep green and glossy.

SPECIAL CONDITIONS Grows on chalk, takes drought, but avoid shade and pollution.

SPECIAL USES As a specimen plant in the heather garden.

Right For rock or heather garden, and tolerating slightly chalky soils, there is the dwarf Scots pine, *Pinus sylvestris* 'Beuvronensis'

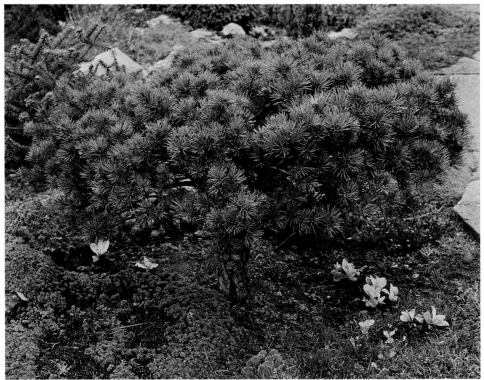

Pinus mugo 'Gnom'
DWARF MOUNTAIN PINE

SHAPE Forms a dome.
SIZE About 60 by 60cm (2 by 2ft) in 10 years; ultimately about 2 by 2m (6 by 6ft).
FOLIAGE Evergreen, long, deep green needles.
SPECIAL CONDITIONS Grows well enough on chalk, but avoid shade and pollution.
SPECIAL USES A useful pine for the rock garden.

Pinus mugo 'Mops'
DWARF MOUNTAIN PINE

SHAPE Forms a rounded bush.
SIZE In 10 years attains about 40 by 60cm (16 by 24in).
FOLIAGE Evergreen, greyish green.
SPECIAL CONDITIONS As for 'Gnom'.
SPECIAL USES Rock garden.

Pinus nigra
AUSTRIAN PINE

SHAPE Young plants are conical; older specimens are umbrella-shaped and lose their lower branches.
SIZE Ultimately 20–40m (66–132ft) in height, with a spread up to half of this.
FOLIAGE Evergreen, deep green.
SPECIAL CONDITIONS Grows on chalk, and ideal for coastal gardens.
SPECIAL USES Used as a windbreak.

Pinus pumila 'Glauca'
DWARF SIBERIAN PINE

SHAPE Rounded or dome shaped.
SIZE In 10 years it will attain about 50cm in height with a spread of 1m (20in by 3ft).
FOLIAGE Evergreen, blue-grey, a rather unusual colour among the pines.
SPECIAL CONDITIONS Must be grown in an open, sunny position, free from pollution.
SPECIAL USES An excellent dwarf pine for the heather garden, associating particularly well with golden foliage varieties.

Pinus strobus 'Nana'
DWARF WEYMOUTH PINE

SHAPE Forms a wide-spreading bush.
SIZE In 10 years a height of 75cm and a spread of 1m (2½ by 3ft). The ultimate size is 2.4 by 3m (8 by 10ft).
FOLIAGE Evergreen, very dense, with a most pleasing overall texture, silvery blue-green, again an unusual colour among dwarf pines.
SPECIAL CONDITIONS Must be grown in an open, sunny position, free from pollution.
SPECIAL USES Highly recommended for the heather garden, particularly striking when grouped with golden heathers.

Pinus sylvestris 'Beuvronensis'
DWARF SCOTS PINE

SHAPE Very compact, forming a dome shape.

SIZE In 10 years will grow to about 75cm in height, with a spread of 1m (2½ by 3ft). Ultimately about 2 by 2m (6 by 6ft).

FOLIAGE Evergreen, grey-green.

SPECIAL CONDITIONS Takes slightly alkaline or chalky soils. Needs an open, sunny position, free from pollution.

SPECIAL USES Grow it either in the heather garden or in a rock garden.

The Totara

Podocarpus nivalis
ALPINE TOTARA

SHAPE Generally a low-spreading shrub.

SIZE Can reach 2m (6ft) in height with a similar spread, although generally much lower.

FOLIAGE Evergreen, the leaves being narrow, leathery and olive-green in colour.

SPECIAL CONDITIONS A very hardy, although little-known conifer, growing well in chalky soils. Avoid very exposed areas as the plant needs shelter from cold, drying winds.

SPECIAL USES A good conifer for the rock garden.

The Swamp Cypress

Taxodium distichum
SWAMP CYPRESS

SHAPE A very graceful tree, forming a broad cone.

SIZE Ultimately 30–50m (100–165ft) in height, with a spread of about one-third of this.

FOLIAGE Deciduous, ferny appearance, bright green, turning bronze in autumn before it falls. The fibrous red-brown bark on the trunk and branches is most attractive.

SPECIAL CONDITIONS Needs damp or wet soil, ideally by the side of a pool or lake, although it is not essential to plant it near water. An acid or lime-free soil is best.

SPECIAL USES As a specimen tree — say, in a lawn or by the side of a pool or lake.

The Yews

Taxus baccata
COMMON YEW

SHAPE Variable, normally used as a hedging plant.

SIZE Hedges can be grown to a height of 1.8–2.4m (6–8ft).

FOLIAGE Evergreen, very dense and dark green.

SPECIAL CONDITIONS Very hardy, growing well in heavy shade. Ideal for chalky soils; the drainage must be good.

SPECIAL USES It makes a fine formal hedge.

Taxus baccata 'Fastigiata Aurea'
GOLDEN IRISH YEW

SHAPE Forms a very narrow column.

SIZE Attains a height of about 2m (6ft) in 10 years; ultimately 4–5m (14–17ft) in height.

FOLIAGE Evergreen, yellow-green, the best colour being when new growth is forming in the spring and early summer.

SPECIAL CONDITIONS Needs full sun for the best colour.

SPECIAL USES Makes a superb specimen plant for a lawn, or for a tub. Can also be recommended for a mixed group of conifers, and to give height in the heather garden.

Taxus baccata 'Repandens'
DWARF FORM OF COMMON YEW

SHAPE Forms a low, wide-spreading specimen.

SIZE Ultimately 50cm in height with a spread of 3m (20in by 10ft).

FOLIAGE Deep green.

SPECIAL CONDITIONS As for *T. baccata*.

SPECIAL USES Suitable for the rock garden, good as ground cover.

Taxus baccata 'Summergold'
FORM OF THE COMMON YEW

SHAPE Semi-prostrate.

SIZE In 10 years it will attain a height of about 50cm with a spread of 1.2m (20in by 4ft).

FOLIAGE Evergreen, yellow, very bright in the summer.

SPECIAL CONDITIONS Needs full sun, otherwise as for *T. baccata*.

SPECIAL USES An excellent ground-cover conifer.

Below The golden Irish yew, *Taxus baccata* 'Fastigiata Aurea', really comes into its own in winter

65

The White Cedars

Thuja occidentalis
WHITE CEDAR

SHAPE Used as a hedging plant, making a fine formal hedge.

SIZE Hedges can be grown to a height of 1.8–2.4m (6–8ft).

FOLIAGE Evergreen, highly aromatic, carried in flattened sprays, deep green.

SPECIAL CONDITIONS Very adaptable and extremely hardy.

SPECIAL USES Excellent for hedges.

Thuja occidentalis 'Danica'
FORM OF THE WHITE CEDAR

SHAPE Globe shaped, very compact.

SIZE In 10 years it will attain no more than 45cm in height and 60cm across (18 by 24in).

FOLIAGE Evergreen, very dense, deep green, turning bronze in the winter.

SPECIAL CONDITIONS As for *T. occidentalis*.

SPECIAL USES Ideal for the heather bed, rock garden or in mixed groups of dwarf conifers.

Thuja occidentalis 'Rheingold'
FORM OF THE WHITE CEDAR

SHAPE Broad cone or dome shaped.

SIZE In 10 years it will be about 1m high and 1.5m wide (3 by 5ft). Ultimately height and spread will be about 3m (10ft).

FOLIAGE Evergreen, deep gold in summer, turning deep coppery gold in winter. Superb for winter colour.

SPECIAL CONDITIONS As for *T. occidentalis*, but full sun needed for best foliage colour.

SPECIAL USES Ideal for a mixed group of small conifers, and superb in the heather garden, especially in association with winter-flowering heathers. Probably one of the most popular dwarf conifers of all time.

Thuja occidentalis 'Sunkist'
FORM OF THE WHITE CEDAR

SHAPE Forms a pyramid.

SIZE A slow grower; a maximum height in 10 years of 1.2m (4ft).

FOLIAGE Evergreen, brilliant gold all the year round.

SPECIAL CONDITIONS As for *T. occidentalis*, but full sun needed for best foliage colour.

SPECIAL USES This recently introduced conifer is being recommended for the heather bed and for mixed groups of small conifers.

The Arbor-vitae

Thuja orientalis 'Aurea Nana'
CHINESE ARBOR-VITAE

SHAPE Dome shaped, very neat and compact.

SIZE Attains a height of about 75cm (2½ft) in 10 years; ultimate height and spread 1.5–2m (5–6ft).

FOLIAGE Evergreen, carried in flat erect sprays; in summer bright gold, in winter yellow or bronzy green.

SPECIAL CONDITIONS Adaptable, but needs full sun for best foliage colour.

SPECIAL USES Mixed group of small conifers or heather garden.

Thuja orientalis 'Rosedalis'
CHINESE ARBOR-VITAE

SHAPE Forms a dome shape.

SIZE In 10 years attains 45–50cm (18–20in) in height; ultimately 75cm to 1m (2½–3ft) in height and spread.

FOLIAGE Evergreen, very soft and feathery; in spring bright yellow, in summer light green, and in winter purplish brown.

SPECIAL CONDITIONS Full sun recommended.

Below The foliage of *Thuja orientalis* 'Rosedalis' changes colour with the seasons – here it's early summer

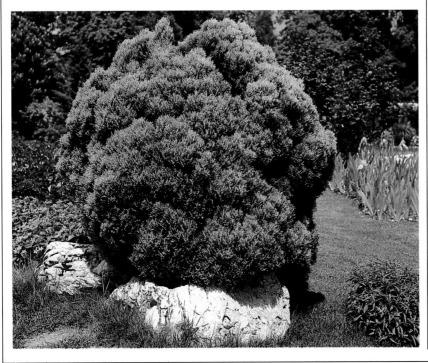

SPECIAL USES Superb in the heather garden, especially when planted with winter-flowering heathers. Also useful in a mixed group of small conifers to provide contrast in colour and texture.

The Western Red Cedars

Thuja plicata
WESTERN RED CEDAR

SHAPE Grown as a formal hedge or as a screen.

SIZE Fast grower: hedges can be 1.8–2.4m (6–8ft) in height; screens very much higher.

FOLIAGE Evergreen, pleasantly aromatic (fruity), carried in flat sprays, deep green and glossy.

SPECIAL CONDITIONS Best in moist soils, but will succeed in dry and alkaline conditions.

SPECIAL USES Hedges, screens and windbreaks. The variety 'Atrovirens' is specially recommended for hedges.

Thuja plicata 'Stoneham Gold'
DWARF WESTERN RED CEDAR

SHAPE Forms a globe-shaped bush.

SIZE Growing to 75cm (2½ft) in height and spread in 10 years; ultimately 2 by 2m (6 by 6ft).

FOLIAGE Evergreen, very deep golden-yellow, tinted bronze. Good colour all the year round, and highly recommended for winter colour.

SPECIAL CONDITIONS As for *T. plicata*, but full sun needed for best foliage colour.

SPECIAL USES Ideal for the heather garden or mixed groups of small conifers.

Thuja plicata 'Zebrina'
VARIETY OF THE WESTERN RED CEDAR

SHAPE Forms a broad cone.

SIZE In 10 years will reach a height of about 3m (10ft); ultimately 15–20m (50–65ft), with a spread of about one-third of this.

FOLIAGE Evergreen, pale green striped with yellow, the best colour being in early summer.

SPECIAL CONDITIONS As for *T. plicata*.

SPECIAL USES An excellent specimen conifer for the lawn, but also recommended for mixed groups of larger conifers.

The Hemlocks

Tsuga canadensis 'Bennett'
FORM OF EASTERN HEMLOCK

SHAPE Semi-prostrate, with arching branches, but flat topped.

SIZE In 10 years 30cm in height with a spread of 75cm (12in by 2½ft); ultimately 1m high by 2m (3 by 6ft).

FOLIAGE Evergreen, medium green.

SPECIAL CONDITIONS Needs a moist yet well-drained soil; succeeds in shade.

SPECIAL USES For the heather garden or a mixed group of small conifers.

Tsuga heterophylla
WESTERN HEMLOCK

SHAPE Grown as a hedge — it makes an excellent formal hedge.

SIZE Can be grown as a hedge to a height of 1.8 to 2.4m (6–8ft).

FOLIAGE Evergreen, rather like yew, dense, dark green.

SPECIAL CONDITIONS Not suited to chalky soils — needs moist, deep loamy soil. Thrives in partial shade.

SPECIAL USES For hedges.

Below Chamaecyparis lawsoniana 'Pembury Blue' contrasting beautifully with Thuja plicata 'Zebrina'

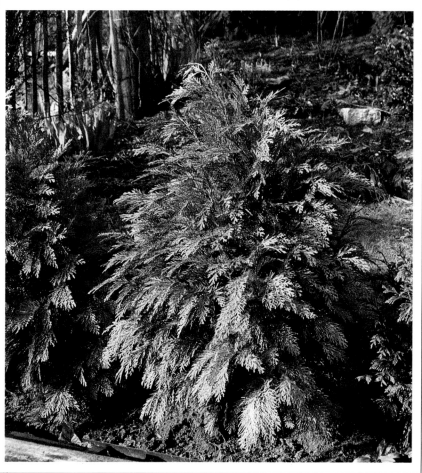

CHAPTER SEVEN

HEATHERS FOR ALL SEASONS

Opposite Heathers growing with other carefully chosen plants, including hardy perennials and shrubs

IT IS POSSIBLE to have heathers in flower all the year round. To illustrate this, these descriptive lists have been grouped into flowering seasons: that is, spring, summer, autumn and winter. These, respectively, embrace the months February to May, June to September, September to November, and December to February. These are fairly rough groups, to give you a general idea of flowering seasons; sometimes flowering overlaps into adjacent groups. However, the exact flowering period is given for each species or variety listed.

Heights have been given for each species or variety. These are the heights to expect when the plants are in flower (except in the case of tall plants, such as tree heaths, when the ultimate height of the plant has been given). Spreads have been given only for large heaths and heathers, such as the tree heaths. The other heaths and heathers generally have a spreading habit of growth and the spreads can be variable. Also, they are generally planted in groups of each variety for bold effect. Therefore, as is the normal practice, I have instead

Right One of the tree heaths, *Erica Arborea* 'Alpina', with sweetly scented flowers in March and April

suggested a suitable number of plants per m² (square yard). These planting densities will result in a bold effect within a comparatively short period of time.

SPRING

*Erica arborea
TREE HEATH

GENERAL HABIT Forms a very bushy upright specimen.

SIZE At least 3.6m in height with a spread of 1.8–2.4m plus (12 by 6–8ft).

FLOWERS The blooms, which appear in March and April, are white, deliciously fragrant and very attractive to bees.

FOLIAGE A very attractive feature of this tree heath, being bright green.

SPECIAL CONDITIONS Acid soil is needed. The plant is not usually fully hardy in Britain, and is therefore recommended only for mild areas. Plants should be staked after planting until well established.

SPECIAL USES Primarily for the heather garden, and very useful for giving height to an otherwise rather flat planting scheme. The variety 'Alpina' is also recommended and is hardier than the species. The foliage is bright green and the flowers even more sweetly scented.

Erica australis
SPANISH HEATH, SOUTHERN TREE HEATH

GENERAL HABIT Upright, with a rather spreading habit of growth.

*Has colourful or otherwise attractive foliage.

Above Erica x darleyensis 'Darley Dale' grows well on chalk and blooms from November to April

SIZE About 1.8m high by 1.2m across (6 by 4ft).

FLOWERS The tubular, scented, rosy purple blooms are produced in April and May.

FOLIAGE Deep green.

SPECIAL CONDITIONS Acid soil needed, but plants will take very slight alkalinity. Plants easily damaged by snow and wind.

SPECIAL USES Recommended for giving variation in height in the heather garden. The variety 'Mr Robert' is also recommended, being hardier and with white flowers.

Erica x *darleyensis* 'Jack H. Brummage'
WINTER-FLOWERING HEATHER

GENERAL HABIT A rounded, very bushy habit of growth.

SIZE Height is about 45cm (18in). Three plants per m² (sq yd).

FLOWERS Red-purple with deep brown stamens, appearing February to March — really starting at the tail-end of winter.

FOLIAGE This is quite attractive, the young shoots in spring being yellow.

SPECIAL CONDITIONS Grows well in chalky soils.

SPECIAL USES An excellent ground-cover plant in the heather garden or elsewhere.

Erica erigena (E. mediterranea) 'Brightness'
MEDITERRANEAN HEATH

GENERAL HABIT Bushy, compact and upright.

SIZE Height 1m (3ft). Three plants per m² (sq yd).

FLOWERS Purplish red, appearing in the period March to May.

FOLIAGE Deep green, with attractive bronze tips in the winter.

SPECIAL CONDITIONS Will thrive in chalky soils but does not relish very dry conditions.

SPECIAL USES For extra height in the heather garden.

Erica erigena (E. mediterranea) 'Golden Lady'
MEDITERRANEAN HEATH

GENERAL HABIT Bushy, with a neat, rounded shape.

SIZE 60cm (2ft) high. Plant three to the m² (sq yd).

FLOWERS White, not too freely produced, May.

FOLIAGE This is the main attraction, being brilliant golden-yellow all the year round.

SPECIAL CONDITIONS Takes chalky soil, provided that it is not too dry.

SPECIAL USES Ideal for foliage contrast in the heather garden or shrub border.

Erica erigena (E. mediterranea) 'Irish Dusk'
MEDITERRANEAN HEATH

GENERAL HABIT A large spreading plant.

SIZE Height 60cm (2ft). Two plants only per m² (sq yd).

FLOWERS Pink blooms from salmon-pink buds, appearing between November and May.

FOLIAGE Pale grey, a pleasing background for the flowers.

SPECIAL CONDITIONS Takes chalky soils provided that they are not too dry.

SPECIAL USES Mainly used in heather beds and gardens.

Erica erigena (E. mediterranea) 'W. T. Rackliff'
MEDITERRANEAN HEATH

GENERAL HABIT Bushy, forming a neat, rounded shape.

SIZE Height 60cm (2ft). Three plants per m² (sq yd).

FLOWERS Large white blooms are produced in March and April.

FOLIAGE This is attractive, being bright green, a good background for the flowers.

SPECIAL CONDITIONS Takes chalky soil so long as it is not too dry.

SPECIAL USES Mainly used in heather beds and gardens.

Erica herbacea (E. carnea) 'Ann Sparkes'
WINTER-FLOWERING HEATHER

GENERAL HABIT Spreading — forms mats of growth.

SIZE Growing to 20cm (8in) high. Five plants per m² (sq yd).

FLOWERS Deep purple-red, appearing in February and March.

FOLIAGE This is one of the main attractions, as it is orange-yellow with bronze-red tips.

SPECIAL CONDITIONS As with all *E. herbacea* varieties thrives in chalky soil provided it is not too thin.

SPECIAL USES A highly recommended variety, giving excellent foliage colour in heather beds or mixed borders.

Erica herbacea (E. carnea) 'Aurea'
WINTER—FLOWERING HEATHER

GENERAL HABIT A spreading, mat-forming plant.

SIZE Growing to 20cm (8in) high. Five plants per m² (sq yd).

FLOWERS This is a very free-flowering variety, the deep pink blooms appearing in the period February to April.

FOLIAGE Another attraction: the leaves are golden yellow.

SPECIAL CONDITIONS Grows well in chalky soils.

SPECIAL USES Highly recommended for summer foliage effect, either in a heather garden or in association with dwarf conifers and other small shrubs.

Erica herbacea (E. carnea) 'Foxhollow'
WINTER-FLOWERING HEATHER

GENERAL HABIT Prostrate habit and a vigorous grower.

SIZE Growing to 15cm (6in) high. Three plants per m² (sq yd) as it spreads well.

FLOWERS Lavender flowers, not too freely produced, between February and April.

FOLIAGE This is the major attraction: in summer it is bright gold, and in winter tinted with red.

SPECIAL CONDITIONS Grows well in chalky soils.

SPECIAL USES A marvellous heather for foliage effect, especially with dwarf conifers in a heather bed. Also useful with small shrubs in a mixed border.

Erica herbacea (E. carnea) 'Loughrigg'
WINTER-FLOWERING HEATHER

GENERAL HABIT Very vigorous, with an upright habit of growth.

SIZE Height 20cm (8in). Five plants per m² (sq yd).

FLOWERS Deep pink-purple, produced in February and March.

FOLIAGE Deep green, turning bronze in the winter.

SPECIAL CONDITIONS Grows in chalky soils.

SPECIAL USES This is a highly recommended variety, best used in the heather bed or garden.

Erica herbacea (E. carnea) 'Myretoun Ruby'
WINTER-FLOWERING HEATHER

GENERAL HABIT Forms neat mats of growth.

SIZE Growing to 20cm (8in) high. Five plants per m² (sq yd).

FLOWERS Ruby red, appearing between February and April.

FOLIAGE Deep green, forming a superb background for the flowers.

SPECIAL CONDITIONS Grows well in chalky soils.

SPECIAL USES Lovely as ground cover around winter or early spring flowering shrubs, such as witch hazels (hamamelis) or forsythia.

Below Erica erigena 'Brightness', a variety of the Mediterranean heath, attains about 1m (3ft) in height and flowers from March to May

Erica herbacea (E. carnea) 'Ruby Glow'
WINTER-FLOWERING HEATHER

GENERAL HABIT Spreads quite vigorously, but nevertheless neat and compact overall.

SIZE Growing to 20cm (8in) high. Five plants per m² (sq yd).

FLOWERS Ruby red, produced in March and April.

FOLIAGE Deep green, an excellent background for the flowers.

SPECIAL CONDITIONS Grows well in chalky soils.

SPECIAL USES Very highly recommended; suggested use as for 'Myretoun Ruby'.

Erica herbacea (E. carnea) 'Westwood Yellow'
WINTER-FLOWERING HEATHER

GENERAL HABIT Prostrate, vigorous but nevertheless overall compact habit.

SIZE Height 15cm (6in). Five plants per m² (sq yd).

FLOWERS Extremely free flowering, lavender, February to April.

FOLIAGE The main attraction, being golden yellow.

SPECIAL CONDITIONS Suitable for chalky soils.

SPECIAL USES Once this becomes better known it is sure to prove a popular variety. Looks good with dwarf conifers in the heather garden, especially those with greyish or bluish foliage.

Below Flowering between January and March is *Erica* x *veitchii* 'Exeter', useful for providing height in the heather garden

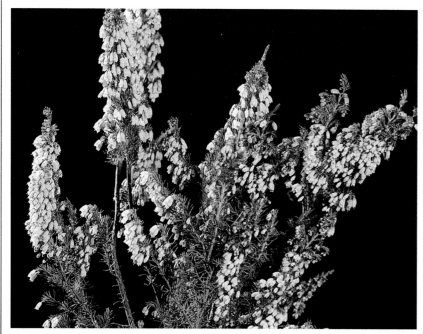

Erica lusitanica
PORTUGAL OR TREE HEATH

GENERAL HABIT Erect habit of growth with feathery branches.

SIZE Height 3m, spread 1m (10 by 3ft).

FLOWERS White blooms coming from pink buds, well scented, being produced in the period December to May in 6–8cm (2–3in) long racemes.

FOLIAGE Most attractive, being light green and feathery.

SPECIAL CONDITIONS Should really be grown in acid soils, but will thrive in very slightly alkaline conditions. Plants may be cut back by hard frosts, but generally new shoots appear in the spring.

SPECIAL USES It is suggested that this species is grown in the heather garden to give height and variation in foliage texture. Would also look good in a mixed shrub border.

Erica umbellata
PORTUGUESE HEATH

GENERAL HABIT An erect, branched species.

SIZE Up to 1m (3ft) in height with a spread of about half this.

FLOWERS These appear in May and June, and are deep pink with prominent dark brown anthers.

FOLIAGE Medium green and feathery, creating a very attractive texture.

SPECIAL CONDITIONS This moderately tender heath can be grown in chalky soils. Best suited to milder counties in Britain.

SPECIAL USES Best in the heather garden to give height and variation in foliage texture.

Erica x *veitchii* 'Exeter'
TREE HEATH

GENERAL HABIT A very vigorous and tall species.

SIZE Growing to 2.4m in height with a spread of about 1m (8 by 3ft).

FLOWERS The white, scented flowers are carried in plumes between January and March.

FOLIAGE Bright green and feathery.

SPECIAL CONDITIONS Needs acid or lime-free soil. Only hardy in the south-west of England.

SPECIAL USES Generally grown in the heather garden, where it will provide height and variation in foliage texture. Also a suitable heather for a mixed or shrub border.

SUMMER

Calluna vulgaris 'Alba Plena'
LING

GENERAL HABIT A quick-growing variety forming quite dense growth.

SIZE Height 50cm (20in). Five plants per m² (sq yd).

FLOWERS Double white blooms are very freely produced during August and September.

FOLIAGE Medium green.

SPECIAL CONDITIONS Must have acid or lime-free soil.

SPECIAL USES An excellent variety for the heather garden. The flowers are good for cutting for indoor arrangements.

Calluna vulgaris 'Alportii'
LING

GENERAL HABIT Tall and upright habit of growth.

SIZE Growing to 60cm (2ft) high. Five plants per m² (sq yd).

FLOWERS Bright crimson and very freely produced during August and September.

FOLIAGE Deep green, becoming even deeper in the winter.

SPECIAL CONDITIONS Must have acid or lime-free soil.

SPECIAL USES Generally grown in the heather garden. Looks good with grey-leaved or golden heathers or conifers.

Calluna vulgaris 'Anne Marie'
LING

GENERAL HABIT A bushy compact variety.

SIZE Height 25cm (10in). Five plants per m² (sq yd).

FLOWERS The blooms open pale pink and then deepen to deep rose. They appear between August and October.

FOLIAGE Deep green.

SPECIAL CONDITIONS Must have acid or lime-free soil.

SPECIAL USES Highly recommended for the heather garden.

Calluna vulgaris 'Beoley Gold'
LING

GENERAL HABIT Fairly bushy habit but not as dense as some.

SIZE Height 30–40cm (12–15in). Five plants per m² (sq yd).

FLOWERS The flowering period is

Above The flowers of *Calluna vulgaris* 'Anne Marie' open pale pink and then deepen to deep rose

August and September but the white blooms are not freely produced.

FOLIAGE The main attraction, bright gold all the year round.

SPECIAL CONDITIONS Acid or lime-free soil is essential.

SPECIAL USES This is an excellent foliage plant, looking good in the heather garden, for instance with bluish or greyish conifers. Also makes a good splash of colour in a shrub border.

Calluna vulgaris 'Blazeaway'
LING

GENERAL HABIT Rather a loose open habit of growth.

SIZE Height 50cm (20in). Five plants per m² (sq yd).

FLOWERS Mauve blooms are produced in August and September.

FOLIAGE In the summer it is green, but becomes rich red and orange in the winter.

SPECIAL CONDITIONS Needs acid or lime-free soil.

SPECIAL USES This is a plant essentially for winter foliage effect: particularly eye-catching against a background of snow. Try planting it round winter-flowering shrubs and evergreens, as well as in the heather garden, perhaps with dwarf conifers.

Calluna vulgaris 'Boskoop'
LING

GENERAL HABIT Low compact habit of growth.

SIZE Height 30cm (12in). Five plants per m^2 (sq yd).

FLOWERS Lavender blooms produced during August and September.

FOLIAGE Gold-orange, tinted red in the winter.

SPECIAL CONDITIONS Acid or lime-free soil required.

SPECIAL USES Ideal for the heather garden where it creates interest both in summer and winter.

Calluna vulgaris 'County Wicklow'
LING

GENERAL HABIT Forms a compact mound of growth.

SIZE Height 25cm (10in). Five plants per m^2 (sq yd).

FLOWERS The attractive pink double flowers are produced in profusion during August and September.

FOLIAGE Deep green, contrasting well with the flowers.

SPECIAL CONDITIONS Needs acid or lime-free soil.

SPECIAL USES A highly popular variety of ling and should be in every heather garden.

Calluna vulgaris 'C. W. Nix'
LING

GENERAL HABIT This variety has upright stems.

SIZE Height is 60cm (2ft). Five plants per m^2 (sq yd).

FLOWERS The deep crimson spikey blooms are produced in August and September.

FOLIAGE Deep green, make a good background for the flowers which are dark.

SPECIAL CONDITIONS Needs an acid or lime-free soil.

SPECIAL USES Generally planted in the heather garden. Combines well with grey-leaved heathers or conifers.

Calluna vulgaris 'Darkness'
LING

GENERAL HABIT An erect compact habit of growth.

SIZE Height is 45cm (18in). Five plants per m^2 (sq yd).

FLOWERS Extremely free flowering, producing bright crimson blooms during August and September.

FOLIAGE Deep green, the flowers showing up well against it.

SPECIAL CONDITIONS An acid or lime-free soil is needed.

SPECIAL USES A highly recommended variety for the heather garden, combining well with grey-leaved heathers or conifers.

Calluna vulgaris 'Elsie Purnell'
LING

GENERAL HABIT An open habit of growth.

SIZE Height 53cm (21in). Plant five to the m^2 (sq yd).

FLOWERS The rose-pink double flowers are produced in August and September.

FOLIAGE Grey-green, lovely in combination with the flowers.

SPECIAL CONDITIONS Acid or lime-free soil required.

SPECIAL USES A very popular variety for the heather garden.

Calluna vulgaris 'Gold Haze'
LING

GENERAL HABIT Rather loose and open.

SIZE Height 50cm (20in). Five plants per m^2 (sq yd).

Below Calluna vulgaris 'Gold Haze' has good foliage colour all the year round, and white flowers in summer

FLOWERS Produces long sprays of white flowers in August and September.

FOLIAGE Bright golden all the year round.

SPECIAL CONDITIONS Needs acid or lime-free soil.

SPECIAL USES An excellent all-round variety, ideal for the heather garden for summer flowers and for winter foliage effect. Try combining it with greyish or bluish conifers. Also looks good as ground cover round evergreen shrubs — say, in a mixed or shrub border. The flowers are also suitable for cutting for indoor arrangements.

Calluna vulgaris 'Golden Carpet'
LING

GENERAL HABIT A prostrate, mat-forming variety of slow growth.

SIZE Height 15cm (6in). Due to its slow rate of growth, six plants per m² (sq yd) is a suitable density.

FLOWERS The reddish purple blooms are produced in August and September.

FOLIAGE In the summer the foliage is golden and in winter turns orange-red.

SPECIAL CONDITIONS Needs lime-free or acid soil.

SPECIAL USES Although the flowers are attractive, this variety is used mainly for foliage effect in the heather garden. Due to its slow rate of growth it can also be recommended for small containers such as window boxes.

Calluna vulgaris 'Goldsworth Crimson'
LING

GENERAL HABIT Starts off fairly compact but becomes straggly in time.

SIZE Height is 80cm (31in). Five plants per m² (sq yd).

FLOWERS The deep crimson blooms are produced from August to October, but this variety may be shy of flowering on some soils.

FOLIAGE The deep green leaves make a good background for the dark blooms.

SPECIAL CONDITIONS Acid or lime-free soil is needed.

SPECIAL USES This fairly old variety is generally included in the heather garden.

Calluna vulgaris 'J. H. Hamilton'
LING

GENERAL HABIT Of vigorous habit, forms a low spreading mat.

SIZE Height is 25cm (10in). Five plants per m² (sq yd).

FLOWERS The bright pink double flowers are carried in spikes during August and September, when it makes a truly spectacular display.

FOLIAGE The deep green foliage makes a good background for the flowers.

SPECIAL CONDITIONS Acid or lime-free soil required.

SPECIAL USES This is one of the best varieties of ling, and justifiably very popular. Plant it at the edge of the heather garden or bed. The flowers are excellent for cutting.

Calluna vulgaris 'Joy Vanstone'
LING

GENERAL HABIT A tallish but neat grower.

SIZE Height 50cm (20in). Five plants per m² (sq yd).

Above Calluna vulgaris 'Joy Vanstone', whose golden foliage turns deep orange in the winter

Left One of the most popular varieties of *Calluna vulgaris* is 'Elsie Purnell', blooming late summer

Above The foliage is the major feature of *Calluna vulgaris* 'Robert Chapman' and it changes with the seasons

FLOWERS In August and September bright pink flowers are produced.

FOLIAGE Golden, turning deep orange in winter.

SPECIAL CONDITIONS Needs an acid or lime-free soil.

SPECIAL USES Highly recommended for winter foliage effect, either in the heather garden or in a shrub border.

Calluna vulgaris 'Kinlochruel'
LING

GENERAL HABIT Forms a compact mound.

SIZE Height 25cm (10in). Six plants per m² (sq yd) to ensure fairly quick ground cover.

FLOWERS Double white blooms produced in August and September.

FOLIAGE Deep green.

SPECIAL CONDITIONS Needs acid or lime-free soil.

SPECIAL USES A suitable variety for small containers such as window boxes and tubs, as well as for the heather garden.

Calluna vulgaris 'Mair's Variety'
LING

GENERAL HABIT A strong, vigorous grower, which becomes straggly after some years.

SIZE Height is 75cm (2½ft). Four plants per m² (sq yd).

FLOWERS White, carried in very tall spikes during August and September.

FOLIAGE Medium green.

SPECIAL CONDITIONS Needs acid or lime-free soil.

SPECIAL USES Despite its rather straggly habit after some years, this is nevertheless considered a superb variety. It makes an excellent display in heather beds and gardens, and associates well with other shrubs in a mixed border. The flowers are ideal for cutting for indoor arrangements.

Calluna vulgaris 'Mullion'
LING

GENERAL HABIT Well-branched and semi-prostrate.

SIZE Height 20cm (8in). Five plants per m² (sq yd).

FLOWERS Deep pink, appearing in August and September.

FOLIAGE Medium green, can be damaged by frosts in winter.

SPECIAL CONDITIONS Needs lime-free or acid soil.

SPECIAL USES This is an excellent ground-cover plant, to be used either in the heather garden or in mixed borders or shrub beds.

Calluna vulgaris 'Multicolor'
LING

GENERAL HABIT A dwarf, compact ling.

SIZE Height is 15cm (6in). Planting density is seven plants per m² (sq yd).

FLOWERS Purple, produced in the period July to September.

FOLIAGE Various colours, changing with the seasons: yellow, orange, bronze and red.

SPECIAL CONDITIONS Acid or lime-free soil.

SPECIAL USES An excellent variety for winter foliage effect. With its neat, compact habit it would be suitable for permanent planting in small containers, such as window boxes.

Calluna vulgaris 'Orange Queen'
LING

GENERAL HABIT Forms a neat, rounded bush.

SIZE Height 40cm (15in). Five plants per m² (sq yd).

FLOWERS Lavender blooms are produced in August and September.

FOLIAGE This ling is essentially grown for its attractive foliage. In spring it is golden-yellow, in summer it turns orange, while in autumn and winter it assumes an even deeper orange hue.

SPECIAL CONDITIONS Acid or lime-free soil is needed.

SPECIAL USES An excellent ling for winter foliage effect, either in the heather garden or round winter-flowering shrubs and evergreens.

Calluna vulgaris 'Robert Chapman'
LING

GENERAL HABIT A very dense habit of growth.

SIZE Height is 40cm (16in). As the spread is not great set six plants to the m² (sq yd).

FLOWERS Purple, produced during August and September.

FOLIAGE The foliage is the major feature of this ling, as it is very colourful and changes with the seasons: first it is gold, then bronze, and finally red and yellow.

SPECIAL CONDITIONS Acid soil needed.

SPECIAL USES One of the best lings for winter foliage effect, and consequently highly popular. For planting suggestions see 'Orange Queen'. The effect is particularly striking against a background of snow.

Calluna vulgaris 'Schurig's Sensation'
LING

GENERAL HABIT Strong but compact.

SIZE Height 40cm (15in). Five plants per m² (sq yd).

FLOWERS Bright rose-pink produced from August to November.

FOLIAGE Medium green.

SPECIAL CONDITIONS Acid or lime-free soil required.

SPECIAL USES An outstanding and very hardy ling for the heather garden.

Calluna vulgaris 'Serlei'
LING

GENERAL HABIT Forms a tall upright bush.

SIZE Height 60cm (24in). Five plants to the m² (sq yd).

FLOWERS White, carried in long sprays from August to October.

FOLIAGE Bright medium green.

SPECIAL CONDITIONS Needs acid or lime-free soil.

SPECIAL USES A useful addition to the heather garden, the flowers being especially recommended for cutting for use in indoor arrangements.

Calluna vulgaris 'Silver Knight'
LING

GENERAL HABIT Has a very compact habit of growth.

SIZE Height is 30cm (12in). Five plants per m² (sq yd).

FLOWERS Pink, appearing in August and September.

FOLIAGE The silvery woolly foliage is an attractive feature.

SPECIAL CONDITIONS Acid or lime-free soil.

SPECIAL USES Particularly recommended for foliage contrast in the heather garden — try it with golden-leaved varieties, or with deep green foliage.

Calluna vulgaris 'Silver Queen'
LING

GENERAL HABIT Low, bushy and compact.

SIZE Height 25cm (10in). Five plants per m² (sq yd).

FLOWERS Purple, August and September, but not too freely produced.

FOLIAGE The silver-grey woolly foliage is attractive.

SPECIAL CONDITIONS Acid or lime-free soil and unpolluted air.

SPECIAL USES As for 'Silver Knight'.

Below The silvery woolly foliage of *Calluna vulgaris* 'Silver Knight' is an attractive feature

Right A superb combination of foliage and flower colour – *Calluna vulgaris* 'Sister Anne', of prostrate habit

Calluna vulgaris 'Sir John Charrington'
LING

GENERAL HABIT Quite a tall variety when in flower and fairly wide-spreading.
SIZE Height is 40cm (15in). Three plants per m² (sq yd).
FLOWERS Deep crimson appearing in August and September.
FOLIAGE Gold-orange, but in winter tinted with red.
SPECIAL CONDITIONS Acid soil needed.
SPECIAL USES A useful dual-purpose variety, with colour in summer and winter. Grow it in the heather garden or shrub border.

Calluna vulgaris 'Sister Anne'
LING

GENERAL HABIT Prostrate and compact.
SIZE Growing to 10cm (4in) high. Seven plants per m² (sq yd).
FLOWERS Pink, very freely produced in August and September.
FOLIAGE Grey and woolly — very distinctive.
SPECIAL CONDITIONS Acid or lime-free soil needed.
SPECIAL USES A highly popular, truly excellent variety. Ensures foliage contrast in the heather garden. Plant in a bold group for best effect.

Calluna vulgaris 'Sunset'
LING

GENERAL HABIT A loose habit of growth.
SIZE Height 30cm (12in). Five plants per m² (sq yd).
FLOWERS Pink, August and September, but not very freely produced.
FOLIAGE The attractive feature, for the leaves are gold, yellow and orange.
SPECIAL CONDITIONS Acid soil needed.
SPECIAL USES Excellent variety for foliage effect in winter.

Calluna vulgaris 'Tib'
LING

GENERAL HABIT Vigorous, upright and compact.
SIZE Growing to 30–60cm (12–24in) high. Five plants per m² (sq yd).
FLOWERS Rose-red, double, very freely produced from July to October.
FOLIAGE Deep green.

SPECIAL CONDITIONS Acid or lime-free soil.
SPECIAL USES A highly recommended variety which should be in every heather bed. Also suitable for small containers.

Calluna vulgaris 'Wickwar Flame'
LING

GENERAL HABIT A low, compact variety.
SIZE Height 30cm (12in). Five plants per m² (sq yd).
FLOWERS Lavender, August and September.
FOLIAGE In summer it is orangy yellow, and in winter bright orangy red.
SPECIAL CONDITIONS Acid or lime-free soil.
SPECIAL USES Summer and winter foliage colour in the heather bed or shrub border.

Daboecia cantabrica
ST DABEOC'S HEATH

GENERAL HABIT Shrubby, branching habit of growth.
SIZE Up to 1m (3ft) high with a similar spread. Generally planted, however, at three to five plants per m² (sq yd).
FLOWERS Large, bell-shaped, purplish pink, May to October.
FOLIAGE Elliptic, hard, pointed, deep green, silvery below.
SPECIAL CONDITIONS Acid or lime-free, moist soils.
SPECIAL USES Generally grown in the heather garden but also looks at home in a shrub border.

Daboecia cantabrica 'Alba'
ST DABEOC'S HEATH

GENERAL HABIT As species.
SIZE Height 60cm (2ft). Five plants per m² (sq yd).

FLOWERS Large, bell-shaped, white, freely produced from June to October.
FOLIAGE As species.
SPECIAL CONDITIONS Acid and moist soils needed.
SPECIAL USES As species.

*Daboecia cantabrica 'Atropurpurea'
ST DABEOC'S HEATH

GENERAL HABIT As species.
SIZE Height 60cm (2ft). Five plants per m² (sq yd).
FLOWERS Large, bell-shaped, deep purple, June to October.
FOLIAGE Green, flushed bronze.
SPECIAL CONDITIONS Acid and moist soil.
SPECIAL USES As species.

*Daboecia cantabrica 'Bicolor'
ST DABEOC'S HEATH

GENERAL HABIT As species.
SIZE Growing to 60cm (2ft) high. Five plants per m² (sq yd).
FLOWERS White, pink-purple, or striped, June to October.
FOLIAGE As species.
SPECIAL CONDITIONS Acid and moist soil.
SPECIAL USES As species.

*Daboecia cantabrica 'Porter's Variety'
ST DABEOC'S HEATH

GENERAL HABIT Upright and compact.
SIZE Height 15cm (6in). Five plants per m² (sq yd).
FLOWERS Small, pinkish purple, June to October.
FOLIAGE As species.
SPECIAL CONDITIONS Acid and moist soils.
SPECIAL USES As species.

*Daboecia cantabrica 'Praegerae'
ST DABEOC'S HEATH

GENERAL HABIT As species, but vigorous.
SIZE Height 30cm (12in). Five plants per m² (sq yd).
FLOWERS Deep pink, in long, arching spikes, June to October.
FOLIAGE Bright medium green.
SPECIAL CONDITIONS Acid and moist soils; avoid exposed situations.

SPECIAL USES As species; highly recommended.

*Daboecia cantabrica 'William Buchanan'
ST DABEOC'S HEATH

GENERAL HABIT Vigorous, yet compact.
SIZE Growing to 30cm (12in) high. Five plants per m² (sq yd).
FLOWERS Crimson, very freely produced from June to October.
FOLIAGE Deep glossy green.
SPECIAL CONDITIONS Acid and moist soils.
SPECIAL USES As species.

Erica ciliaris 'Mrs C. H. Gill'
DORSET HEATH

GENERAL HABIT Low growing, upright shoots.
SIZE Height up to 30cm (12in). Four to five plants per m² (sq yd).
FLOWERS Clear red, freely produced from July to October.
FOLIAGE Deep green.
SPECIAL CONDITIONS Needs acid or lime-free soil.
SPECIAL USES Varieties of the Dorset heath are a major feature of most heather gardens.

Below Daboecia cantabrica, St Dabeoc's heath, has a shrubby branching habit and large flowers

Right Erica cinerea 'Atrosanguinea', a variety of the bell heather, is indispensable in the heather garden

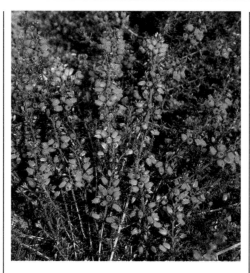

Erica ciliaris 'Stoborough'
DORSET HEATH

GENERAL HABIT A strong-growing variety.

SIZE Growing to 60cm (2ft) high. Four to five plants per m² (sq yd).

FLOWERS Pearly white, in long spikes, July to October.

FOLIAGE Bright green.

SPECIAL CONDITIONS Needs acid or lime-free soil.

SPECIAL USES As for 'Mrs C. H. Gill'; an excellent variety.

Erica cinerea 'Alba Minor'
BELL HEATHER

GENERAL HABIT Stiff and branching, but compact.

SIZE Growing to 15cm (6in) high. Five plants per m² (sq yd).

FLOWERS White, freely produced from June to October.

FOLIAGE Light green.

SPECIAL CONDITIONS Needs acid soil but can take drier soils than most cinereas.

SPECIAL USES Varieties of bell heather are indispensable in the heather garden.

Erica cinerea 'Atrorubens'
BELL HEATHER

GENERAL HABIT Spreading habit of growth.

SIZE Growing to 15–20cm (6–8in) high. Five plants per m² (sq yd).

FLOWERS Bright red in long sprays, freely produced from July to September.

FOLIAGE Medium green.

SPECIAL CONDITIONS As for 'Alba Minor'.

SPECIAL USES As for 'Alba Minor'.

Erica cinerea 'Atrosanguinea Smith's Variety'
BELL HEATHER

GENERAL HABIT Low, spreading habit.

SIZE Growing to 15–20cm (6–8in) high. Five plants per m² (sq yd).

FLOWERS Scarlet, very freely produced from June to September.

FOLIAGE Deep green.

SPECIAL CONDITIONS As for 'Alba Minor'.

SPECIAL USES As for 'Alba Minor'. One of the best varieties.

**Erica cinerea* 'C. D. Eason'
BELL HEATHER

GENERAL HABIT Forms a shapely bush.

SIZE Growing to 30cm (12in) high. Five plants per m² (sq yd).

FLOWERS Brilliant reddish pink in dense spikes, July to September.

FOLIAGE Very dark green and attractive.

SPECIAL CONDITIONS As for 'Alba Minor'.

SPECIAL USES As 'Alba Minor'. An outstanding variety.

Erica cinerea 'Cevennes'
BELL HEATHER

GENERAL HABIT Upright growth.

SIZE Height 22–30cm (9–12in). Five plants per m² (sq yd).

FLOWERS Lavender-rose, very freely produced from July to September.

FOLIAGE Bright, pale green.

SPECIAL CONDITIONS As 'Alba Minor'.

SPECIAL USES As 'Alba Minor'.

**Erica cinerea* 'Cindy'
BELL HEATHER

GENERAL HABIT Strong, upright grower.

SIZE Growing to 15–20cm (6–8in) high. Five plants per m² (sq yd).

FLOWERS Glowing purple, July to September.

FOLIAGE Dark bronzy green.

SPECIAL CONDITIONS As 'Alba Minor'.

SPECIAL USES As 'Alba Minor'.

**Erica cinerea* 'Golden Drop'
BELL HEATHER

GENERAL HABIT Prostrate.

SIZE Height 15cm (6in) when in flower.

Five plants per m² (sq yd).

FLOWERS Pink, not very freely produced. June to August.

FOLIAGE The main attraction: in summer coppery gold, in winter reddish.

SPECIAL CONDITIONS As 'Alba Minor'.

SPECIAL USES One of the best cinerea varieties for foliage effect.

Erica cinerea 'Hockstone White'
BELL HEATHER

GENERAL HABIT A strong, upright grower.

SIZE Growing to 45cm (18in) high. Four plants per m² (sq yd).

FLOWERS White, carried in long spikes from July to October.

FOLIAGE Bright green.

SPECIAL CONDITIONS As 'Alba Minor'.

SPECIAL USES As 'Alba Minor'. One of the best white varieties.

Erica cinerea 'Pink Ice'
BELL HEATHER

GENERAL HABIT Rounded, very compact and bushy.

SIZE Growing to 25cm (10in) high. Five

plants per m² (sq yd).

FLOWERS Bright pink, June to September.

FOLIAGE Bright deep green, tinted bronze in late winter and spring.

SPECIAL CONDITIONS As 'Alba Minor'.

SPECIAL USES As 'Alba Minor'. A highly rated variety.

Below Erica cinerea 'Golden Drop' in summer. In the winter the foliage becomes reddish

Erica cinerea 'P. S. Patrick'
BELL HEATHER

GENERAL HABIT A strong grower.

SIZE Growing to 25cm (10in) high. Five plants per m² (sq yd).

FLOWERS Bright purple in long spikes, from June to September.

FOLIAGE Deep green and glossy.

SPECIAL CONDITIONS As 'Alba Minor'.

SPECIAL USES As 'Alba Minor'. Another highly rated variety.

Erica cinerea 'Purple Beauty'
BELL HEATHER

GENERAL HABIT Vigorous and bushy.

SIZE Growing to 25cm (10in) high. Five plants per m² (sq yd).

FLOWERS Bright purple, very freely produced from July to September.

FOLIAGE Deep green.

SPECIAL CONDITIONS As 'Alba Minor'.

SPECIAL USES As 'Alba Minor'.

Erica cinerea 'Rock Pool'
BELL HEATHER

GENERAL HABIT Prostrate.

SIZE Growing to 15cm (6in) high. Five plants per m² (sq yd).

FLOWERS July and August, but not noteworthy.

FOLIAGE The main attraction, it is deep gold, changing in winter to copper-bronze.

SPECIAL CONDITIONS As 'Alba Minor'.

SPECIAL USES As 'Alba Minor'.

Erica cinerea 'Stephen Davis'
BELL HEATHER

GENERAL HABIT A neat, low grower.

SIZE Growing to 15cm (6in) high. Six plants per m² (sq yd).

FLOWERS Bright magenta, June to September.

FOLIAGE Deep green.

SPECIAL CONDITIONS As 'Alba Minor'.

SPECIAL USES As 'Alba Minor'.

Erica cinerea 'Velvet Night'
BELL HEATHER

GENERAL HABIT Quite tall and spreading.

SIZE Growing to 30cm (12in) high. Five plants per m² (sq yd).

FLOWERS Deep blackish purple, July and August.

FOLIAGE Medium green.

SPECIAL CONDITIONS As 'Alba Minor'.

SPECIAL USES As 'Alba Minor'. Highly recommended.

Erica cinerea 'Windlebrooke'
BELL HEATHER

GENERAL HABIT Fairly tall and spreading.

SIZE Growing to 25cm (10in) high. Five plants per m² (sq yd).

FLOWERS Purple, not very freely produced, July to September.

FOLIAGE This is most attractive, being pale gold in summer, and becoming orange-red in winter.

SPECIAL CONDITIONS As 'alba Minor'.

SPECIAL USES Particularly recommended for winter foliage effect in the heather garden.

Erica mackaiana 'Lawsoniana'
HEATH

GENERAL HABIT Rather prostrate.

SIZE Growing to 15cm (6in) high. Five plants per m² (sq yd).

FLOWERS Rose-pink, July to September.

FOLIAGE Mid-green.

SPECIAL CONDITIONS Needs acid or lime-free soil.

SPECIAL USES Not very well known, but nevertheless an excellent heath for summer colour in the heather garden.

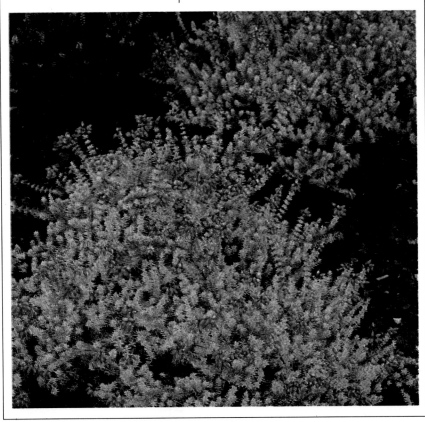

Below The foliage of *Erica cinerea* 'Windlebrooke' is attractive at any time, but becomes orange-red in winter

Erica terminalis (E. stricta, E. corsica)
CORSICAN HEATH

GENERAL HABIT Forms a rigid, upright bush.

SIZE Growing 2.4m high, 1.2m wide (8 × 4ft).

FLOWERS Deep pink, June to September, turning russet-brown when dead, making a pleasing winter feature.

FOLIAGE Bright green when it first emerges, turning deep green, carried in whorls and very dense.

SPECIAL CONDITIONS Excellent on chalk. Stems easily damaged by snow.

SPECIAL USES As a tall specimen plant in the heather garden; can also be used for hedging.

Erica tetralix 'Alba Mollis'
CROSS-LEAVED HEATH

GENERAL HABIT Fairly open, spreading habit.

SIZE Growing to 30cm (12in) high. Five plants per m² (sq yd).

FLOWERS White, June to September.

FOLIAGE Most attractive — silvery grey.

SPECIAL CONDITIONS Acid or lime-free, moist soil is needed. Prefers boggy places in the wild.

SPECIAL USES Makes an excellent foliage plant in the heather garden, especially if associated with golden-leaved heathers. All the *tetralix* varieties listed here are considered the best available.

Erica tetralix 'Con Underwood'
CROSS-LEAVED HEATH

GENERAL HABIT As 'Alba Mollis'.

SIZE Height 25cm (10in). Five plants per m² (sq yd).

FLOWERS Large, crimson, June to October.

FOLIAGE Greyish green.

SPECIAL CONDITIONS As 'Alba Mollis'.

SPECIAL USES As 'Alba Mollis'.

Erica tetralix 'Hookstone Pink'
CROSS-LEAVED HEATH

GENERAL HABIT As 'Alba Mollis'.

SIZE Growing 30cm (12in) high. Five plants per m² (sq yd).

FLOWERS Deep pink, June to October.

FOLIAGE Pale silvery grey.

SPECIAL CONDITIONS As 'Alba Mollis'.

SPECIAL USES As 'Alba Mollis'.

Erica tetralix 'Pink Star'
CROSS-LEAVED HEATH

GENERAL HABIT As 'Alba Mollis'.

SIZE Growing 20cm (8in) high. Five plants per m² (sq yd).

FLOWERS Pink, giving a good, bright effect, June to October.

FOLIAGE Smoky grey, an excellent background for the flowers.

SPECIAL CONDITIONS As 'Alba Mollis'.

SPECIAL USES As 'Alba Mollis'.

Erica vagans 'Cream'
CORNISH HEATH

GENERAL HABIT Vigorous, forms a very dense bush.

SIZE Growing 50cm (20in) high. Five plants per m² (sq yd).

FLOWERS Cream-white, very freely produced from August to November.

FOLIAGE Deep green.

SPECIAL CONDITIONS Will take slightly alkaline soils but best in acid conditions.

SPECIAL USES All of the *vagans* varieties listed here are among the best available and are virtually indispensible for summer colour in the heather garden.

Below The foliage of *Erica tetralix* 'Con Underwood' makes a superb background for the flowers

Right Calluna vulgaris 'H.E. Beale', a superb, well-known variety whose flowers are ideal for cutting

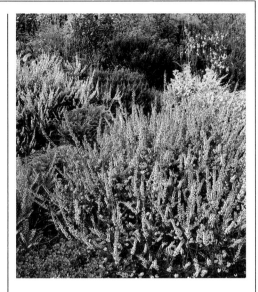

Erica vagans 'Lyonesse'
CORNISH HEATH

GENERAL HABIT A strong grower.
SIZE Growing to 45cm (18in) high. Five plants per m² (sq yd).
FLOWERS White, with conspicuous brown anthers, August to October.
FOLIAGE Bright green.
SPECIAL CONDITIONS As for 'Cream'.
SPECIAL USES As for 'Cream'.

Erica vagans 'Mrs D. F. Maxwell'
CORNISH HEATH

GENERAL HABIT Robust and vigorous.
SIZE Growing to 45cm (18in) high. Five plants per m² (sq yd).
FLOWERS Dark rose-pink with deep brown anthers, August to October.
FOLIAGE Deep green.
SPECIAL CONDITIONS As for 'Cream'.
SPECIAL USES As for 'Cream'.

Erica vagans 'St Keverne'
CORNISH HEATH

GENERAL HABIT Forms a neat, compact bush.
SIZE Growing 50cm (20in) high. Five plants per m² (sq yd).
FLOWERS Rose-pink with deep brown anthers, very freely produced from August to October.
FOLIAGE Deep green.
SPECIAL CONDITIONS As for 'Cream'.
SPECIAL USES As for 'Cream'.

*Erica vagans 'Valerie Proudley'
CORNISH HEATH

GENERAL HABIT Neat, compact, a slow grower.
SIZE Growing 15–20cm (6–8in) high. Six plants per m² (sq yd).
FLOWERS White, August to October.
FOLIAGE Golden, good colour all the year round.
SPECIAL CONDITIONS As for 'Cream'.
SPECIAL USES As for 'Cream'.

*Erica x watsonii 'Dawn'
HEATH

GENERAL HABIT Dense habit of growth.
SIZE Growing to 20cm (8in) high. Five plants per m² (sq yd).
FLOWERS Large, rose-pink, July to October.
FOLIAGE In spring and early summer the tips of the new growths are yellow.
SPECIAL CONDITIONS Needs acid or lime-free soil.
SPECIAL USES An excellent plant for ground cover as it makes very dense growth.

Below A well-known variety of the Cornish heath, Erica vagans 'Mrs D.F. Maxwell' flowers into autumn

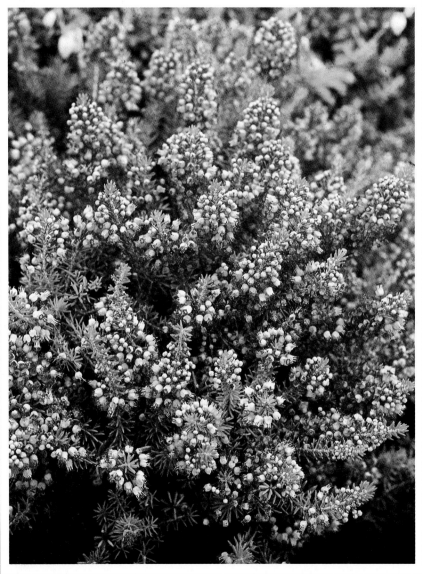

AUTUMN

Calluna vulgaris 'H. E. Beale'
LING

GENERAL HABIT Best flowering occurs on young plants.
SIZE Growing to 60cm (2ft) high. Five plants per m^2 (sq yd).
FLOWERS Silvery pink, double, carried in sprays, September to November.
FOLIAGE Grey-green, with mauvish tints in winter.
SPECIAL CONDITIONS Acid or lime-free soil essential.
SPECIAL USES This is a superb, well-known variety, the flowers being ideal for cutting for indoor arrangements.

Calluna vulgaris 'My Dream'
LING

GENERAL HABIT Erect and branching.
SIZE Growing to 60cm (2ft) high. Five plants per m^2 (sq yd).
FLOWERS Pure white, double, very freely produced in September and October.
FOLIAGE Medium green.
SPECIAL CONDITIONS Acid or lime-free soil essential.
SPECIAL USES Heather garden.

Calluna vulgaris 'Peter Sparkes'
LING

GENERAL HABIT A vigorous grower.
SIZE Height 45cm (18in). Five plants per m^2 (sq yd).
FLOWERS Deep pink, double, carried in dense spikes during September and October.
FOLIAGE Medium green.
SPECIAL CONDITIONS Acid or lime-free soil essential.
SPECIAL USES Heather garden.

WINTER

Erica x *darleyensis* 'Arthur Johnson'
WINTER-FLOWERING HEATHER

GENERAL HABIT A vigorous grower.
SIZE Growing 60–90cm (2–3ft) high

when in flower. Three plants per m^2 (sq yd).
FLOWERS Rose-pink, carried in long spikes from November to May.
FOLIAGE A good shade of green.
SPECIAL CONDITIONS Grows well in chalky soils.
SPECIAL USES An excellent ground-cover plant in the heather garden or shrub border.

Erica x *darleyensis* 'Darley Dale'
WINTER-FLOWERING HEATHER

GENERAL HABIT A vigorous grower.
SIZE Growing 45cm (18in) high. Three plants per m^2 (sq yd).
FLOWERS Pink, very freely produced from November to April.
FOLIAGE Medium to dark green.
SPECIAL CONDITIONS Grows well in chalky soils.
SPECIAL USES Very reliable and widely planted; excellent ground cover in heather garden or shrub border.

Erica x *darleyensis* 'Furzey'
WINTER-FLOWERING HEATHER

GENERAL HABIT spreading habit of growth.
SIZE Growing 45cm (18in) high. Three plants per m^2 (sq yd).

Above Erica x *darleyensis* 'Arthur Johnson' will grow on chalky soils and flowers from November to May

Above Erica x darleyensis 'Silberschmelze' is considered by many to be the finest *darleyensis* variety

Below In spring and early summer the foliage of *Erica* x *darleyensis* 'George Rendall' is tinged cream-pink at the tips

FLOWERS Deep pink, very freely produced from November to April.

FOLIAGE Deep green, tinged red.

SPECIAL CONDITIONS Grows well on chalky soils.

SPECIAL USES Excellent ground cover in heather garden or shrub border.

Erica x *darleyensis* 'George Rendall'
WINTER-FLOWERING HEATHER

GENERAL HABIT Spreading habit of growth.

SIZE Growing to 45cm (18in) high. Three plants per m² (sq yd).

FLOWERS Rich pink, November to March.

FOLIAGE In spring and early summer it is tinged cream-pink at the tips.

SPECIAL CONDITIONS Grows well in chalky soils.

SPECIAL USES Excellent ground cover in the heather garden or shrub border.

Erica x *darleyensis* 'Ghost Hills'
WINTER-FLOWERING HEATHER

GENERAL HABIT Fairly low, spreading habit.

SIZE Growing to 40cm (15in) high. Three plants per m² (sq yd).

FLOWERS Deep pink, very freely produced from November to May.

FOLIAGE The new shoots have attractive cream tips.

SPECIAL CONDITIONS Excellent on chalky soils.

SPECIAL USES Good ground cover in heather garden or shrub border.

Erica x *darleyensis* 'Silberschmelze' ('Molten Silver')
WINTER-FLOWERING HEATHER

GENERAL HABIT Strong, spreading and vigorous.

SIZE Growing to 45cm (18in) high. Three plants per m² (sq yd).

FLOWERS White, carried in very long spikes, November to April.

FOLIAGE Deep green in winter, an excellent background for the flowers.

SPECIAL CONDITIONS Grows well in chalky soils.

SPECIAL USES Considered by many to be the finest x *darleyensis* variety. Excellent ground-cover plant in heather garden or shrub border. A superb companion for dwarf conifers.

Erica herbacea (E. carnea) 'Eileen Porter'
WINTER-FLOWERING HEATHER

GENERAL HABIT Prostrate, spreading mats.

SIZE Growing 20cm (8in) high. Five plants per m² (sq yd).

FLOWERS Bright red, very freely produced from October to April.

FOLIAGE Deep green.

SPECIAL CONDITIONS Grows well in chalky soils.

SPECIAL USES Excellent ground cover in the heather garden or shrub border. Superb planted round winter-flowering shrubs.

Erica herbacea (E. carnea) 'January Sun'
WINTER-FLOWERING HEATHER

GENERAL HABIT A compact, miniature variety.

SIZE Growing to 10cm (4in) high. Six to eight plants per m² (sq yd).

FLOWERS Pink, not too freely produced.

FOLIAGE Golden, the main feature.

SPECIAL CONDITIONS Grows well in chalky soils.

SPECIAL USES Ideal for the rock garden or heather garden, and for small containers such as sink gardens and window boxes.

Erica herbacea (E. carnea) 'King George'
WINTER-FLOWERING HEATHER

GENERAL HABIT A neat, compact

habit of growth.

SIZE Growing to 20cm (8in) high. Five plants per m² (sq yd).

FLOWERS Rose-pink, very freely produced from December to February.

FOLIAGE Deep green.

SPECIAL CONDITIONS Grows well in chalky soils.

SPECIAL USES An old favourite, still highly recommended for the heather garden or for planting round winter-flowering shrubs.

Erica herbacea (E. carnea) 'Pink Spangles'
WINTER-FLOWERING HEATHER

GENERAL HABIT A vigorous, spreading variety.

SIZE Growing to 20cm (8in) high. Three plants per m² (sq yd).

FLOWERS Large, deep pink, very freely produced from January to March.

FOLIAGE Deep green.

SPECIAL CONDITIONS Grows well in chalky soils.

SPECIAL USES Ideal ground cover in heather garden, shrub border or round winter-flowering shrubs and trees.

Erica herbacea (E. carnea) 'Praecox Rubra'
WINTER-FLOWERING HEATHER

GENERAL HABIT Prostrate, forms mats.

SIZE No more than 15cm (6in) high. Five plants per m² (sq yd).

FLOWERS Small, deep rose-red, December to March.

FOLIAGE Medium to deep green.

SPECIAL CONDITIONS Grows well in chalky soils.

SPECIAL USES As for 'Pink Spangles'.

Erica herbacea (E. carnea) 'Springwood Pink'
WINTER-FLOWERING HEATHER

GENERAL HABIT Vigorous, prostrate, forming spreading mats.

SIZE Growing to 20cm (8in) high. Three plants per m² (sq yd).

FLOWERS Pink, freely produced from January to March.

FOLIAGE Deep green.

SPECIAL CONDITIONS Grows well on chalky soils.

SPECIAL USES One of the most popular *herbacea* varieties, used extensively as ground cover in shrub borders, heather gardens and round winter-flowering

trees and shrubs. A good variety for permanent planting in window boxes, perhaps with early-flowering miniature bulbs.

Erica herbacea (E. carnea) 'Springwood White'
WINTER-FLOWERING HEATHER

GENERAL HABIT A very fast grower, forming prostrate mats.

SIZE Growing to 20cm (8in) high. Three plants per m² (sq yd).

FLOWERS White, with brown anthers, from January to March.

FOLIAGE Bright green.

SPECIAL CONDITIONS Grows well in chalky soils.

SPECIAL USES As for 'Springwood Pink'. Takes dry conditions quite well.

*Erica herbacea (E. carnea) 'Vivellii'
WINTER-FLOWERING HEATHER

GENERAL HABIT Forms low, spreading mats.

SIZE Growing to 20cm (8in) high. Five plants per m² (sq yd).

FLOWERS Bright carmine, very freely produced from January to March.

FOLIAGE Deep green, becoming deep bronze in winter.

SPECIAL CONDITIONS Grows well in chalky soils.

SPECIAL USES As for 'Springwood Pink'.

Above An excellent ground-cover plant, *Erica herbacea* 'Springwood White' flowers from January to March

INDEX

Acknowledgements

The publishers would like to thank Squire's Garden Centre, Twickenham and The Chelsea Gardener, Sydney Street, London SW3 for supplying plants and equipment for the cover photograph.

Picture credits

Pat Brindley: 1, 2/3, 15, 23, 25 (t), 46, 50, 62, 75 (t), 78, 80
R. J. Corbin: 18
Derek Gould: 6, 7, 14, 19, 21 (t), 34, 39 (b), 65, 67, 70, 87
Iris Hardwick Library: 27
David Levin: 16
A. Schilling: 21 (b)
Harry Smith Horticultural Photographic Collection: 10, 11, 22, 24 (bl,br), 25 (b), 37, 39 (t), 41, 43, 44, 45 (t,b), 47, 48, 53, 60, 66, 68, 69, 72, 73, 74, 75 (b), 79, 81 (t,b), 84 (t,b), 86 (t,b)
Michael Warren: endpapers, 4, 5, 8, 9, 12, 13, 28, 29, 35, 36, 40, 42, 48/9, 51, 54, 55 (t,b), 56 (t,b), 57, 59, 61 (l,r), 63, 64, 71, 76, 77, 82, 83, 85

Artwork

Johnnie Pau: 26
Richard Phipps: 17, 37
Charles Stitt: 30, 31, 32, 33